Also published by Stanley Thornes (Publishers) Ltd

*Politics*

Chris Leeds, *Politics in Action, contemporary sources for students of politics and government*
J R S Whiting, *Politics and Government, a first sourcebook*
Paul Denham, *Modern Politics*

*Religious Studies*

W Owen Cole, *Six Religions in the Twentieth Century*
Roger Whiting, *Religions of Man*

*Social Studies*

A D Burgen, *Comprehension Exercises in Sociology*
Stephen Moore, *Sociology Alive!*
Roger Whiting, *Crime and Punishment: A Study Across Time*

*History*

Philip Sauvain, *Modern World History 1919 onwards*
W O Simpson, *Changing Horizons: Britain 1914–80*

*General Studies*

J M and A D Burgen, *Focus, Key Concepts in General Studies*

# PEACE AND WAR

## A FIRST SOURCEBOOK

Chris Leeds

Stanley Thornes (Publishers) Ltd

First published in 1987 by:
Stanley Thornes (Publishers) Ltd
Old Station Drive
Leckhampton
CHELTENHAM GL53 0DN
England


British Library Cataloguing in Publication Data

Leeds, Christopher A.
    Peace and war: a first sourcebook.
    1. War    2. Peace
    I. Title
    327.1      JX1952
    ISBN 0-85950-526-X

Typeset by Grafikon nv, Oostkamp, Belgium
in 11/13 Baskerville
Printed and bound in Great Britain by R.J. Acford, Chichester

# CONTENTS

# FOREWORD

The political polarisation associated by some with the word 'peace' and allied issues is distressing. Advocates of War Studies or Defence or Conflict Studies are thought to the right-wing, while advocates of Peace Studies are supposed to be members of the left, probably supporters of CND. Having a non-political non-sectarian outlook on this issue myself, and believing that there is no reason intrinsic to the subject of Peace why it should not be studied objectively and every reason why it should be studied seriously by the young, I am glad to recommend Chris Leeds' *Peace and War*. In it he provides a great deal of material which any teacher will find useful and stimulating, and he aims to present this in modern terms and in as balanced a way as possible. It should be a most useful sourcebook for teachers of middle forms in secondary schools.

Michael McCrum
Master, Corpus Christi College
Cambridge

# INTRODUCTION

In most subjects the student is like a novice or mere learner, at the mercy of the expert, since his or her previous knowledge and experience may not be especially relevant. In contrast everyone is able to contribute, whether individually or at a group level, to a course covering the themes of Peace and War. Their own ideas and experiences at home, in the community and in life generally may be important to the topic being studied.

Virtually all subjects cover some ideas or topics relevant to Peace and Conflict and so can be used as mediums for teaching in this area. Alternatively Peace and Conflict may be taught as a special subject. Peace is also associated with a certain form of behaviour and a learning environment which is democratic and participatory rather than authoritarian.

This **Activity-based Book** aims to encourage every student to contribute positively to the success of any course by providing a range of resource material and questions, projects or problem-solving exercises. It is primarily intended for the 14–16 age-group, and the material can be used for both exam and non-exam studies. While the book should be of particular interest to English-speaking students throughout the world, the intention is that it will also be helpful for adults working for a peaceful world or interested in the dimensions of peace and war as a subject, and in schools or colleges where English is studied as a foreign language.

The book is broadly divided into two parts. Part I deals mainly with problems and conflicts, while Part II looks at remedies and solutions. Chapter I contains basic core material for an understanding of the book. The parts containing examples of forms of conflict from press cuttings should be used as a basis of reference when studying other chapters.

Chapter I starts with forms of conflict at the personal and small group level, and broader or larger conflicts are discussed in Chapters 2–6. Chapters 7–8, at the start of Part II, deal with peacemaking at the individual level, and how individuals can help promote peace. The subsequent chapters cover peace at the national and international levels.

The book emphasises that certain problems are many-sided, with people differing about their nature, causes and solutions. Certain extracts try to persuade the reader to support a particular policy of opinion. Controversial issues, e.g. nuclear weapons, the Cold War, and questions involving morals or 'values' such as human rights, are also part of a course in Peace and Conflict. Ideally the student is encouraged not the be 'closed-minded' (automatically favouring one view while ignoring others). A student should strive to be fair or objective, acquiring the skill of distinguishing fact from opinion or propaganda, and of studying an issue or problem from different angles. Then he or she is better equipped to form an opinion. However the reader need not take objectivity to the extreme lengths of always looking at another point of view in cases where his conscience, instinct or intelligence indicates that one path is correct and proper. (See the cartoon below.)

Many new topics in schools are related to the themes of Conflict or Peace Studies, including World Studies, Multicultural Education, Development Education, Environmental Studies and Human Rights Education. Elements from these areas of study are included in this book, and they share with Conflict and Peace Studies as one of their aims to help people take a more active part in the development of themselves, their community, their country and the world.

*"And now, in the interests of BALANCE..."*

Private Eye, *10 August 1984*

# ACKNOWLEDGEMENTS

The author and publishers are grateful to the following for permission to reproduce previously published material:

The Associated Press for an extract from 'An Alternative Carpenter in Zimbabwe' by Michelle Faul

Philip Barker for 'Or Not at All?'

Frank Barnaby for an extract from 'UNA's great responsibility', New World – *Disarmament Development and SS D2*, ed. F Boyd, UN Publications

Jane Blewitt for an extract from 'What will it take to prevent nuclear war', Center Focus, Center for Concern, Washington DC

Der Bundesminister der Verteidigung for extracts from the White Paper, *The Security of the Federal Republic of Germany*, 1983

Centre for Global Education for extracts from *World Studies Journal*, Vol. 5, No. 3, 1985

The Controller of Her Majesty's Stationary Office for an extract from a Government pamphlet, Arms Control and Disarmament Unit

Alexander Croal for material in *Friends of the Earth Newspaper*, Summer 1985, Survival 2000

The *Daily Telegraph* for extracts from various editions of their newspapers

André Deutsch Ltd. for an extract from *How to be God* by George Mikes, 1986

*The Economist* for material edition, 16.7.77

*Glasgow Herald* for heading edition, 10.5.86

*The Guardian* for material from various editions of their newspaper

Hugh Hanning for an extract from *United Nations Peacekeeping – 40 Years on and the Way Ahead*, International Peace Academy Inc., 1985

Harmony Music Ltd. for an extract from 'What did you learn at school today?' by Tom Paxton, © 1964 Harmony Music Ltd.

David Higham Associates Ltd. on behalf of Herbert Read for 'The Happy Warrior'

Independent Television Publications Ltd. for extracts from 'Our Teenagers' thoughts about nuclear war', *Television Times*, 10–16 December 1983. Data from Business Decisions Ltd. (1983)

Lenono/Chappell Music Ltd., London, for an extract from 'Imagine' by John Lennon, © 1971 Lenono Music Ltd.

London Express News and Features Services for various extracts from editions of the *Star*, *Daily Express* and *Sunday Express*

*Los Angeles Times* for extract from 'Taming a Savage Beast', 16.4.72

Mail Newspapers plc for extracts from various editions of the *Daily Mail*

The National Center for Public Policy Research for an extract from *The Price of Peace* by Brian Crozier (1983)

National Spiritual Assembly of the Bahá'ís of the United Kingdom for extracts from 'Universality, Human Rights, Peace'

*New Internationalist* for extracts from the May 1983 edition

*The Observer* for extracts from various editions

One World Trust for 'The Elephant' from *Learning for change in a World Society*, ed. R Richardson, 1976, World Studies

Peace News for material based on *'An Introduction to Social Defense'* and an extract from *Peace News*

*Punch* for extracts from 5.3.69 edition

Queensland Police Department for extracts from their publications

*Radio Times* for an extract from 'From Nepal to the Palace' by G Leon, 1–7 June 1985

Stockholm International Peace Research Institute and Cambridge University Press for diagrams adapted from *SIPRI Yearbook* (1982) and used in *The Arms Race* by John Turner, CUP, 1983

Syndication International Ltd. for material from various editions of the *Daily Mirror*

Times Newspapers Ltd. for extracts from various editions of *The Times*

Ted Trainer for an extract from *'The Limits to Growth'*, 1984

Peter Viggers, MP for extracts from material published by the Campaign For Defence and Multilateral Disarmament

The World Bank for data from *World Development Report 1986*, Oxford University Press Inc.

The World Conservation Strategy for an extract from material published in March 1980. Copyright of WWF, IUCN and UNEP (1980)

World Disarmament Campaign for material from their publications

We also wish to thank the following who have provided photographs and illustrations and permission to reproduce them:

Alder/*The Sunday Times*, 18 November 1984 (p. 9); Associated Press (p. 65); © Auth 1986 Universal Press Syndicate (p. 60); BBC Hulton Picture Library (p. 47); © Benson 1986 Tribune Media Services (p. 89); Brookes/*The Sunday Times*, 17 February 1980 (p. 195); Campaign for Defence and Multilateral Disarmament (p. 104); Cummings/Express Newspapers (pp. 105, 171, 182); The Economist (p. 197); Feiffer (p. 73); Friends of the Earth (p. 69); Freedom House, New York (p. 183); Garland/*Daily Telegraph* (pp. 190, 200); Les Gibbard (p. 150); Giles/Express Newspapers (pp. 38, 125); Greenpeace (p. 64); Charles Griffin/*Daily Mirror* (p. 80); *The Guardian* (p. 13); Her Majesty's Stationary Office (p. 103); Holmes McDougall Ltd. (pp. 21, 36); Trevor Hussey/*Peace News* (p. 147); Trevor Hussey/*The Pacifist* (p. 154); Imperial War Museum (pp. 30, 78); Jensen/*Spectator* (p. 15); John Hillelson Agency (p. 120); Ian Kellas (p. 208); John Kent (p. 164); Lowry/*Private Eye* (p. 000); Murray/*Punch* (p. 43); *New Internationalist* (pp. 3, 81); Newman/*Private Eye* (p. 18); New York State Historical Association, Cooperstown, USA (pp. iii,

203); Novosti Press Agency (p. 35); © Oliphant 1983 Universal Press Syndicate (p. 44); Dai Owen/CND Publications Ltd (p. 155); Peace Pledge Union (p. 77); Plantu/Éditions Alain Moreau (p. 180); Popperfoto (p. 93); Neville Pyne (p. 93); Quaker Peace and Service (pp. 97, 196); Radical Statistics Nuclear Disarmament Group (p. 99); Erica Rothenberg (p. 155); Steadman/*Punch* (p. 206); Syndication International (p. 94); Dr F E Trainer (p. 59); United Nations (p. 71); United Nations/Richard Wilson (p. 160); Peter Vujakovic/World Development Movement (p. 59); War Resisters' International (p. 118); World Disarmament Campaign (p. 116); World Priorities (p. 99).

The cover picture is of soldiers in Lisbon, Portugal, in 1974.
Photo: Michelle Gineis (by courtesy of Rex Features).

Every attempt has been made to contact copyright holders, but we apologise if any have been overlooked.

# 1 CONFLICT AT THE PERSONAL LEVEL AND IN SMALL GROUPS

## 1.1 Basic Conflicts

**What is conflict?**   In ordinary language the word 'conflict' is often associated with a violent physical act, for example someone hitting someone else, or with wars, but it also covers other situations. Examples of conflict include:

**Disputes**   We often quarrel with our friends, relatives, or people at school or at work. This conflict is usually shown by harsh or unpleasant, or sometimes insulting words which may be used at the height of an argument. It might also take the form of people being difficult or uncooperative.

**Competition or rivalry**   This exists everywhere in life. We might compete with others to gain the friendship of someone of the opposite sex, to win in a sports contest or to be successful in a career. Shops and other businesses rival each other in terms of price, quality of service and product to gain customers and increase their sales and profit. In Western democracies political parties contend against each other at elections to gain the support of those eligible to vote.

**Violent conflicts**   These differ from disputes in that the aim is to physically harm, injure or kill your opponent, or even an innocent person involved, as occurs during riots, acts of terrorism and wars.

**Useful versus harmful conflict**   Some form of conflict, like the air we breathe, is everywhere and is a vital part of a free society. Conflict implies that we are all different individuals entitled to our own opinions. A peaceful environment can exist with a fair amount of healthy conflict, for example in terms of disagreements about the need for changes to society. However, too much conflict or disagreement can lead to the collapse of a society and chaos. A degree of co-operation and of 'pulling together' is also necessary if a society is to progress and improve, or even remain the same. Healthy or useful conflict can provide ways of coping with life's problems, or alternatives to the use of violence and aggression. (These aspects are discussed in Chapter 7, see pages 123–4.)

# Conflicts of Interest and Value

Two basic forms of conflict are conflict of interest and conflict of value.

**Conflicts of interest** These occur about things people want for themselves, their family or their group (see examples below).

Two or more people or groups may quarrel with each other because they all want the same thing which is in short supply, for example land and food as has happened in many past wars. Others struggle for better jobs, or for power in society, or to be chosen leader of a country in preference to possible rivals.

Some groups have been called interest groups as they work to defend and promote the interests of their members. Trade unions are examples of interest groups, as are professional organisations such as the Law Society and the British Medical Association.

Francis I and I are in complete agreement.

We both want Milan.

*Emperor Charles V*

## THE GAME OF LIFE

Life is just a game. And as in most games there is a scoring system. In football it's called goals, in rugby tries, cricket runs, bridge points. In life there is also a scoring system. It's called money. Whoever amasses the most pounds, dollars, roubles, rupees or yen is adjudged the winner. It's simple, innit?

*Leon Griffiths*, Arthur Daley's Guide to Doing it Right!

The territorial instinct is thought by some to be near-universal. When one animal invades the space of another of the same species the defences are roused. The behaviour may be different – the stickleback turns red with rage and puffs out his chest, the stag roars and struts – but the intention is the same.

The human defends his or her chosen space just as energetically; whether it is the 'egocentric bubble' of personal space that we create around us or the gaily-painted front door that guards family territory.

Our invisible personal bubble excludes all but intimitate and trusted friends. It allows us to keep people literally at arms length. You can feel it threatened in a train when a stranger asks 'is someone sitting here?' making you move the elaborate wall of coat, scarf and bag you have constructed on the seat beside you. You can feel it when a handshake lasts too long, when someone stands too near at a party.

Most social animals are the same: a row of pigeons will continually jostle to balance their feather-filled bubbles on a rooftop; a shoal of silver fish will hang perfectly spaced apart in a patch of warm water. For animals which have to live in a group to survive the bubbles make for a peaceful life.

According to zoologist Desmond Morris the neighbourhood ghettos, working-men's clubs, football stadiums, street corners, public bars and golf clubs each represent remnants of our ancient tribal hunting and gathering territories.

At the national level it is only when we feel our national boundaries threatened that our patriotic tribal identities flower into fully blown territorial aggression. It is then that the exhortation to 'fight them on the beaches' arouses a passionate response. And few people think it strange that grown men and women should consider it perfectly reasonable to kill and be killed defending those beaches.

But territorial disputes in the animal kingdom almost never end in bloodshed. In fact there is seldom even an argument: deterrence in this sense really works. And where simple threat fails to deter a would-be invader, the combat that results is usually brief and bloodless.

*Each person creates their own bubble of personal space. In some cultures the bubbles are much bigger than others.*

Forever Blowing Bubbles, *Debbie Taylor*, New Internationalist, *May 1983*

**Conflicts of value**   These concern matters which might affect not only the individuals or groups involved in the conflict but also many others as well. Certain pressure groups have been called cause groups because they claim they benefit others as well as their members. This distinguishes them from interest groups. Examples of cause groups are Shelter, Greenpeace, Oxfam, the RSPCA, the Child Poverty Action Group and the Campaign for Nuclear Disarmament.

Other examples of value conflicts are:

**1.**   disagreement between political parties about what is best for the individual, sections of society and the country as a whole.

**2.**   differences between religions (for example Christianity, Islam, Buddhism) and within religions (for example the Christian Church is divided into numerous denominations).

**3.**   East—West differences concerning, for example, human rights and how an economy should be managed (see Chapters 5, 6 and 11).

**4.**   North—South differences concerning the best way the developing or poorer countries can be helped (see Chapter 4).

**Basic needs and rights**   Disputes about such matters are often the cause or origin of many violent disturbances in a country, or of civil and international wars (see Chapter 5).

Four important categories of needs and rights are listed below. People often try to get or achieve them for themselves, sometimes to the disadvantage of others, so this list can reflect conflicts of interest. People may also try to obtain such needs and rights for others, for example the poor and underprivileged, so the list also reflects conflicts of value.

Usually people try to achieve the most basic needs first (1 and 2), followed by 3 and 4.

**1.   The means to survive or live** – food and water, materials to make clothing, shelter, energy (for warmth and cooking), space and comfort.

**2.   Security or safety for oneself, family and possessions.**

**3.   Social esteem and social contact** – respect, friendship or love of others, and acceptance by others as a member of various groups.

**4.   Personal success** – some people attain their ambitions in life by making lots of money, others by a career of service helping the unfortunate, whether as doctors, nurses, social workers or through voluntary work for an agency such as the Red Cross.

If a person comes from a family which has little money or influence, he or she might need to struggle more to get on in life compared to the children of the rich and powerful. His or her chances might be improved if the country has an extensive welfare system with cheap or free educational or health facilities. Access to these have been called economic rights or social rights. The person's chances might also be improved if there is a system of civil liberties, or political rights, such as:

- the right to write and speak freely.
- the right to vote in free elections.
- the right to practise any religion.
- the right to enter and leave the country.

## The Level and Scale of a Conflict

**The level of a conflict**  The main levels of conflict are shown in the diagram below.

Stress and emotional problems can be an important element in personal conflict, which is covered in more detail in the next section (1.2) and in Chapter 7. Notice that the diagram shows that as you move outwards or away from the centre, you are moving to larger or wider conflicts in terms of the number of people, groups or countries involved.

**National and international levels**  Within a country, at the national level, those guilty of illegal or criminal behaviour are eventually caught and punished, because there is an organised police force and a legal system. In contrast, at the international level there is no regular police force or army able to catch or stop culprits, whether they are countries, groups or individuals, who break international law. United Nations peacekeeping forces are usually only involved in trying to prevent a serious outbreak of violence or war (see Chapter 10).

Levels of conflict

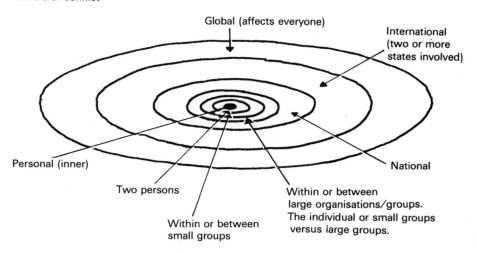

5

Any decision by the International Court of Justice at The Hague in the Netherlands cannot be enforced if any of the persons, groups or countries involved refuse to accept it.

**The worsening of a conflict**   A conflict escalates or increases in scale, that is gets worse, if one or more of the following happens:
- it moves from an inner to an outer level (see diagram), involving more people, groups or countries;
- it moves from non-violent to increasingly violent methods, for example at first it could be a verbal dispute, then a fist fight, then clubs or guns are used.

---

# ACTIVITIES

1. Answer true or false to each of the following:

   (a) If a tenant is arguing with his landlord about how much his rent should be this is a conflict of value.

   (b) If two dogs are fighting for the same bone this illustrates a conflict of interest.

   (c) A tennis tournament represents a harmful form of conflict.

   (d) The group called Friends of the Earth are a cause group rather than an interest group.

   (e) The right to vote in an election is an example of a social right.

2. In which circle of the diagram showing levels of conflict would you place each of the following:

   (a) Urban riots in Britain in 1985.

   (b) A dispute between a husband and wife.

   (c) A dispute between a taxpayer and the Inland Revenue.

   (d) Rivalry between two local gangs.

   (e) Conflict in Northern Ireland since 1969.

   (f) Hostility between the production and sales departments in a firm.

   (g) A person with a heavy workload affected by a severe headache.

   (h) A dispute between local consumers and local retailers.

   (i) A major nuclear war.

   (j) The Second World War.

3. Select two items from the list in Activity 2 and say why each could be placed under two or more levels at the same time.

4. How would you distinguish between conflict at the small group level and at the large group level? Give examples.

5. Suggest how conflicts at different levels may be linked or related by making up a story of an event. If necessary, make use of any of the following:

(a) Sleeplessness            (h) Strike
(b) Frustration              (i) National emergency
(c) Inferiority              (j) Loss of wide support
(d) Dispute with a friend    (k) Desire for glory and success
(e) Failing an exam          (l) International crisis
(f) Divorce                  (m) War.
(g) Overwork

6. Find examples of the 'egocentric bubble' of personal space, mentioned in the article by Debbie Taylor, from experiences in your daily life. In what way does Taylor distinguish sharply between the behaviour of human beings and the behaviour of animals.

7. <u>Dispute</u>     <u>Incompatibility</u>          <u>Friction</u>     <u>Strife</u>
   Old age                                      Illness
   Gun fight                                    Verbal insults
   Starvation                                   Unemployment
   Pride                                        Loutish/yobbish behaviour
   Price war between two oil companies          Mountaineering
   Organised singing contest                    Racial discrimination
   Free elections

(a) Find out the exact meanings of the words underlined above. Which one do you think comes closest to describing the essence of conflict?

(b) With what forms of conflict are the words not underlined associated?

(c) Which of the above are associated with destructive (harmful) and which with creative (constructive) conflicts?

(d) Identify the items above which violate in some way the four categories of basic needs and rights listed on page 4. (You may refer to the section on human rights in Chapter 11, page 178.)

8. Illustrate, by writing down a short imaginary dialogue, how an argument between two people can escalate in terms of the type of words or language used. Use examples from words of emotive appeal or insults, but avoid vulgar language.

# 1.2 Personal, Domestic and Generation Conflict

## Personal, or Inner Conflict and Stress

**Personal, or inner conflict** Inner worries or anxieties frequently concern how we relate to the rest of the world. If we have high expectations of achieving things and then experience many disappointments, whether in studies, work, sport or anything else, this is one cause. We might, on the other hand, just suffer from some feeling of inadequacy or lack of self-confidence, and this might spring from something real, such as being small, thin, not attractive to the other sex, or something largely imagined, such as thinking we are too small or unattractive or being too shy or indecisive.

**Stress** This is an important aspect of personal conflict. It might be due to some sudden event, for example the death of a parent, or caused by the build-up of numerous problems, pressures or irritations which gradually get on top of a person. At the extreme, stress takes the form of shock and possibly a nervous breakdown when someone is temporarily unable to cope. There are certain signs or symptoms of stress such as bad temper, sleeplessness, ill-health and certain obvious causes such as overwork, or living under difficult, dangerous or unpleasant conditions for too long.

A person might become unnecessarily sensitive or aggressive if suffering from stress, and he or she may start abusing or annoying others, as shown in the picture of the man brandishing a sword. A certain degree of stress or tension, however, is part of a healthy life, examples being the many challenges in work, social life and sport.

**Hardiness** It is not easy to predict who will suffer from stress and who will be able to cope. The key word is coping since, although many people today are liable to experience stress in some form or another, a great number are able to deal with it adequately or even act as if it did not exist. Examples are leaders and politicians who seem to thrive living very strenuous lives. Hardiness is the word to describe such people, who:

**1.** have commitment or faith in the importance and value of what they are doing, and
**2.** are involved in numerous activities.

Sickness in one form or another is often a result of stress, and about 70 per cent of hospital cases have been attributed to stress in some form. Perhaps the boy in the cartoon is illustrating one coping technique – the ability to 'switch off' as Winston Churchill used to do with numerous 'cat-naps' during the Second World War. On the other hand, he may just be lazy!

# STRESS 'COSTS INDUSTRY AND NHS A FORTUNE'

STRESS at work is costing British industry and the National Health Service a fortune, and autocratic employers are to blame, according to a leading psychologist.

"HE'S OUR STAR PUPIL — INCREDIBLY RELAXED SORT OF CHAP"

Madness to fight outside ourselves when the struggle is within

# 'Stress' blamed for problem children

### By CHRISTOPHER ROWLANDS
### Education Correspondent

BAD behaviour by today's youngsters is mainly the result of stress factors beyond their control, it is claimed.

They face more serious stress problems than previous generations, according to a report on family life to be published next month.

And the blame for much unruly behaviour by the child of the 80s is put squarely on the effects of high unemployment and broken marriages.

Extracts from The Times, *18 November 1983*

# ACTIVITIES

1. Study and compare the two extracts below. Explain what is meant by 'wrath', 'impulsive' and 'folly'. Write one sentence describing a link between these extracts and another sentence explaining how they are linked to the topic of stress.

   > He who is slow to wrath has great understanding, but he who is impulsive exalts folly.
   >
   > *Proverbs 14 : 29*

   > Emotional Immaturity: This is allowing human nature free expression, and allowing the emotions and not reason to dominate the mind. Examples are yelling, loud talking, bursts of temper and rudeness.

2. Suggest three other possible characteristics of a 'hardy' person who can cope with stress in addition to the two listed in the text.

3. Coping strategies.
   **(a)** Causes  **(b)** Symptoms (effects)
   **(c)** Healthy  **(d)** Unhealthy

   Under each of the above four categories place seven of the following 28 items. Some might go under more than one heading.

   1. High blood pressure
   2. Irritable behaviour
   3. Death of a mother
   4. Meditation
   5. Exam worries
   6. Sleeplessness
   7. Developing a new hobby
   8. Moving home
   9. Nail-biting
   10. Active outdoor exercise
   11. Headaches
   12. Excessive eating
   13. Lack of concentration
   14. Careful diet including salads, fruit and brown rice
   15. Crying
   16. Financial problems
   17. Ulcers
   18. Attempted suicide
   19. Girlfriend or boyfriend rejection
   20. Acne
   21. Talking to friend or counsellor
   22. Vandalism
   23. Reckless driving
   24. Holiday
   25. Loneliness
   26. Depression
   27. Arguments with parents
   28. Hooliganism

4. Case Study. Write a short description (about a page) of an experience someone you know has had involving conflict in your community/locality, and mention how it was resolved. An example might be a dispute between a local authority and a house owner over the rates payable. Small groups could exchange ideas and then a class discussion could be held.

# School and Generation Conflict

**Parent-child relationships**  Certain problems tend to occur between parents and their children as the latter reach their teens. Aspects of generation conflict would include misunderstanding and disagreement between parents and children concerning the following:

- What time the children should be in at night.
- Who should decide what kind of clothes or hair styles they should have.
- How the children should be treated. Some teenagers complain that they continue to be treated as if they were much younger, with parents fussing and worrying unnecessarily, and not allowing them enough freedom and individuality.
- Parents failing to understand that things have changed while always reminding children of how things were in their day.

**How to bring children up**  Every parent has his or her own ideas on this subject but the statement below by Dorothy Law Holte might provide some guidelines.

---

*CHILDREN LEARN WHAT THEY LIVE*

If a child lives with criticism he learns to condemn.
If a child lives with hostility he learns to fight.
If a child lives with ridicule he learns to be shy.
If a child lives with shame he learns to feel guilty.
If a child lives with tolerance he learns to be patient.
If a child lives with encouragement he learns to have confidence.
If a child lives with praise he learns to appreciate.
If a child lives with fairness he learns justice.
If a child lives with security he learns to have faith.
If a child lives with approval he learns to like himself.
If a child lives with acceptance and friendship he learns to find
  love in the world.

*Dorothy Law Holte 'Community Building — Stepping Stones to Progress'*

---

1. BEGIN FROM INFANCY to give the child everything he wants. In this way he will grow up to believe that the world owes him a living.

2. WHEN HE PICKS UP BAD WORDS, laugh at him. It will encourage him to pick up 'gutter phrases' that will blow the top of your head off later.

3. NEVER GIVE HIM ANY spiritual training. Wait until he is 21 and then let him decide for himself.

4. AVOID THE USE of the word 'wrong'. It may develop a guilt complex. This will condition him to believe later when he is arrested for stealing a car that society is against him and he is being persecuted.

5. PICK UP EVERYTHING he leaves lying around – books, shoes and clothes. Do everything for him so he will be experienced in throwing the responsibility on to others.

6. LET HIM READ any printed matter he can get his hands on. Be careful the silverware and drinking glasses are sterilised but let his mind feed on garbage.

7. QUARREL FREQUENTLY in the presence of children. Then they won't be too shocked when the home is broken up.

8. GIVE THE CHILD all the spending money he wants. Never let him earn his own. Why should he have things as tough as you had them?

9. SATISFY HIS EVERY CRAVING for food, drink and comfort. See that every desire is gratified. Denial may lead to harmful frustration.

10. TAKE HIS PART against the neighbours, teachers and policemen. They are all prejudiced against your child.

11. WHEN HE GETS into real trouble, apologise for yourself by saying, 'I never could do anything with him'.

*How to Bring up Your Child to be a Juvenile Delinquent, Queensland Police Department*

## Rights at School

The picture shows three of the five pupils expelled from Kingsdale Comprehensive School, Dulwich, following a strike in which they asserted their right to participate in the running of the school.

The mother of one of the students who demonstrated wrote in *The Guardian* on 9 February 1970. 'There seems to me to be a great inconsistency between democracy in England and the dictatorship children live under at school. Our home life contradicts everything Jerry sees in the school-room. At home, ideas fly – we're always discussing social issues and political ideas. . . . The children who want student-staff-community councils ought to be commended for their public spirit, not treated as delinquents or subversives. But since the strike, we've been told that schools children have no rights at all, no right to strike because they're not involved in a wage contract.'

*John Sutcliffe and Philip Lee-Woolf,* Conflict – Living Issues, 1, *1971*

## Domestic Conflict in Marriage

**What brings people together** The two words 'sameness' and 'difference' not only illustrate the importance of keeping a balance in all things, but explain in part why people make friends or how they find their marriage partners. People are often drawn towards each other initially because of common friends or interests or beliefs. They remain interested in each other, however, because their separate skills and experiences help to complement and enrich the other person.

**Unhappy marriages** Frequently children suffer stress and other problems if their parents are unhappily married, or if they divorce. Sometimes parents stay married for the sake of the children, or only separate when the children are older. Alternatively, some children may help in their own way to bring their parents together after a period when a marriage was on the verge of breakdown.

Causes of unhappy marriages and separations might include the following:

- One of the partners might become bored with the relationship and find another lover.
- One or both of the partners may become too absorbed by their jobs or careers and neglect the other partner, the children or family life.
- There may be cultural differences based on religion, nationality, or background.
- One of the partners may become a well-known celebrity or very financially secure in a short time and this may cause jealousy and other problems.
- There may be a need for one of the partners to work for long periods away from home.

# CHILD ABUSE UP 70 pc IN SIX YEARS

**By David Fletcher**
**Health Service Correspondent**

The number of children under 14 who suffer physical abuse, many of them at the hands of their parents, rose from 6,816 to 7,038 last year, the NSPCC said yesterday.

It said there had been a 70 per cent rise in child abuse over the past six years and blamed marital discord, unemployment and debt as the main trigger factor. Sexual abuse accounts for the biggest proportional rise – 11 per cent of cases last year compared with 1 per cent in 1980.

Daily Telegraph, *19 September 1985*

The quality of life                    by Jensen

The Spectator, *1 June 1974*

# ACTIVITIES

1.  Suggest a reason why the couple in the illustrations below solved their dispute so quickly? What might have been the cause of the argument?

2.  List ten forms of unpleasantness, stress or violence which have affected you or your friends in ordinary life. Examples are forms of verbal abuse (for example sarcasm or nagging) and domination of the conversation at mealtimes or of TV viewing by one family member. Outline how you cope or manage – if you do.

3.  List in order of importance five qualities of a happy family.

4.  Suggest ten ways children can contribute to making a happy family, and help in reconciliation between parents who may be on the verge of separation or divorce.

5.  Refer to the extract on page 12 on Juvenile Delinquency when answering these questions. Work in small groups.
    (a) Discuss each point. Each person decides how much he or she agrees or disagrees with the observation.
    (b) Imagine that you are a parent and ask yourself whether you would adopt a different view.

6.  What does the Jensen cartoon (page 15) say about some of the problems of young couples?

7.  Discuss in groups what makes each member feel angry or violent, and how angrily or aggressively he or she actually behaves.

8.  Do procedures or methods exist by which pupils in your school can
    (a) air their grievances
    (b) participate in a modest way in influencing decisions regarding the rules and other things which affect their school life?

9.  List some of the main causes of bullying. (Make use of material in this chapter.) What peaceful means might be used for dealing with bullies? (See material in Chapters 7–9 for coping with conflict.)

# 1.3 Violence, Aggression and Crime

## Relationship between Violence, Aggression and Crime

Although violence, aggression and crime are not inevitably related, they can be said to present a problem for society as a whole, so it is convenient to treat them all in a special section.

It has been suggested that a certain amount of aggression in people is necessary so that they can assert themselves and defend what rightfully belongs to them. Certain writers, such as Robert Ardrey, argue that human beings in this respect are simply behaving as animals do in the wild but that, unlike animals, people can learn to be civilised and develop and improve their ways of living. Others argue that human beings are in some respects worse than animals, since they sometimes engage in deliberately injuring or killing their own species.

In some ways, aggression and violence are close in meaning, since a person can be both verbally or physically aggressive or violent. The word 'aggression' is often used when referring to life in the animal world, and to the start and finish of hostilities in war. It is also used to describe the attitude of one person towards another.

'Violence' has a broader meaning, covering situations such as acute poverty and serious unemployment, and vandalism. (See structural violence, page 18.)

## The Animal World

Many animals do not normally kill members of their species. Struggle for existence for them does not so much resemble human war as the human activity of slaughtering animals for food, competing for markets and materials, and the protection of one's 'kith and kin'. Obviously animals kill to eat or in self-defence or to protect their family. Instead of killing their own kind, each species develops certain tactics to avoid hurting others. For example:
- piranhas fence with their fin tails rather than bite each other with their razor blade teeth.
- male robins sing aggressively.
- rattlesnakes bash heads till one gives in rather than poison each other.

## Forms of Violence

There is by no means common agreement as to how violence can be classified. Each of the categories on page 18 can also be linked to a form of peace, when the aspect of violence has been eliminated.

**Direct violence** – refers to physical harm done by someone directly to himself or to others. This type of violence tends to be dramatic and vivid, and is often well publicised in the press.

**Structural violence** – refers to a situation of injustice where some people have grievances or are oppressed or exploited by governments, organisations or individuals. South African apartheid is an example. Whereas many believe that peace is the absence of war or direct violence, others argue that real peace can only be obtained when both direct and structural violence no longer exist.

**Mental violence** – refers to certain violent emotions or feelings of hate, jealousy or desire for revenge, or attitudes which might lead to direct violence. Verbal abuse comes in this category.

**Environmental violence** – covers forms of damage and vandalism to the natural world including animals, for example pollution and over-whaling. Natural disasters, such as earthquakes and typhoons, come under this heading too, but these are not anyone's fault.

---

Poverty is the worst kind of violence.

*Mahatma Gandhi*

---

Private Eye, *4 October 1985*

**Violence and conflict**   Three of the forms of violence just described – direct, structural and mental – are also closely linked with questions of how conflict occurs or can be solved. Structural violence, for example racial discrimination or tyranny, can lead to the sufferers becoming frightened or angry. Eventually their attitudes or feelings (mental violence) can influence their actual behaviour if fighting takes place (direct violence). In reverse, peace will only occur if the original problem which created the situation causing the conflict is solved, and if people no longer nurse feelings of hatred or desire for revenge. (See the diagram on page 19 and Chapter 10, page 158.)

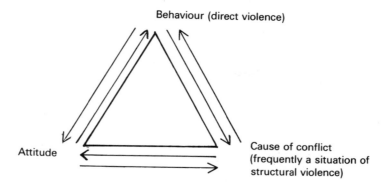

Behaviour (direct violence)

Attitude

Cause of conflict
(frequently a situation of
structural violence)

*The above is adapted from the 'conflict triangle', first popularised by Johan Galtung*

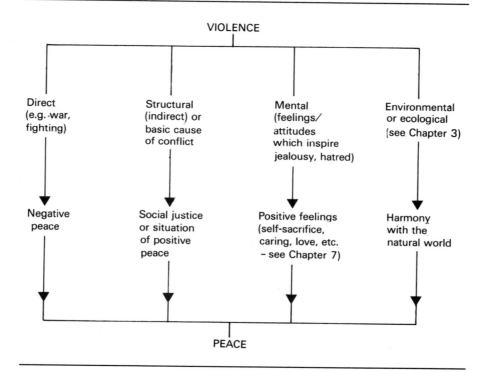

VIOLENCE

Direct
(e.g. war,
fighting)

Structural
(indirect) or
basic cause
of conflict

Mental
(feelings/
attitudes
which inspire
jealousy, hatred)

Environmental
or ecological
(see Chapter 3)

Negative
peace

Social justice
or situation
of positive
peace

Positive feelings
(self-sacrifice,
caring, love, etc.
– see Chapter 7)

Harmony
with the
natural world

PEACE

## The Origins of Violence, Aggression and Crime

**Two opposing views**   There are people who think that individuals are to blame for violence, aggression and crime, others who think that the fault lies with society. Many people, however, believe that some combination of these two views usually presents a truer picture of the origins of violence.

**1.   The individual is to blame**   Supporters of this view tend to think that individuals are responsible for the bad things they do, not society.

According to them, much aggression is basic and natural. People should exercise self-control, otherwise their instincts will get them into trouble, involving breaking rules or laws or being offensive to others. This view maintains that people are not likely to be good or behave well in a society unless there are strong deterrents or punishments which discourage anti-social behaviour and encourage respect for the law and for other people. Violence, crime and war, however, will always be with us, being in the nature of things.

**2. Society is to blame** Supporters of this view tend to believe that individuals are not responsible for bad things they do, but society is. This belief includes the view that people are not born with any natural tendencies which make them good or bad. Each of us has as much potential for tolerance and good as for hatred and evil. A person may become wicked, or aggressive, as a result of bitter experiences gathered from growing up. A tendency towards violent behaviour or crime may result from discontent with a very unpleasant life or working conditions, for example few opportunities, lack of freedom, racism, poverty or unemployment. Advocates of this view recommend changes in the law and basic reforms so as to create a society which is fairer and more just.

**Frustration and scapegoats** If a person or group loses hope of change or fails to get satisfaction from the 'culprit' or 'cause', for example the boss, a landlord or the government, then an outlet or scapegoat for the frustration may be resorted to. This might involve, for example, being rude or unpleasant, or even injuring someone, or damaging property.

**Role of the mass media** In modern life news of any disorder or violence can be communicated almost immediately worldwide. Usually trouble only erupts in areas where a potentially explosive situation exists. However, the mass media, which includes the press and television, may act as an instant fuse, so that disorder in one part of the world might spread elsewhere in a series of 'copycat' situations. For example, the ghetto riots in certain American towns in the 1960s were caused partly by frustration and lack of freedom for non-whites, but they probably became widespread partly as a result of mass media publicity. Black Americans rioted when news and pictures of Martin Luther King's assassination flashed on to television screens.

---

Once the only way for a man to prove his manliness was in war. The gangs of today which destroy property and attack people seemingly without reason are obeying this inherited urge.

*Audrey Whiting,* Daily Mirror, *3 March 1972*

---

# An Evening in Town

CLASP (Crime, Law and Society Project), 1984

# New US mobs rivalling Mafia

**From Christopher Thomas
Washington**

Organized crime in America, though still being dominated by the Mafia, is being transformed by particularly vicious new breeds of prison gangs, ethnic criminal societies, and at least four powerful motor cycle groups with chapters in Europe and Australia.

The Times, *16 March 1986*

---

*Families trapped in rubble*

# 'QUAKE KILLS THOUSANDS'

## Mexico City devastated

Daily Telegraph, *20 September 1985*

---

# KEW GARDENS SHOW SIGN OF ACID RAIN

Daily Telegraph, *25 September 1985*

---

# Salvador bombs sweep guerrillas from their volcano fortress

The Times, *3 April 1986*

---

# Mentally-ill children badly treated in some hospitals

The Times, *3 April 1985*

---

# MILLIONARE GETS LIFE FOR KILLING WIFE

Daily Telegraph, *27 March 1986*

---

# 7 held in 'clean-up soccer' raids

**By John WEEKS, Crime Staff**

CROSSBOWS, swords and a medieval-style spiked iron mace on a chain were among weapons seized by police yesterday in seven raids designed to break up the leadership of a gang of football hooligans.

The Daily Telegraph, *27 March 1986*

---

# Teheran gangs hunt unveiled women

**By Ralph JOSEPH in Athena**

BEARDED Fundamentalists on motor-cycles roared through the streets of Teheran and Isfahan late last week insulting women considered to be unveiled or improperly veiled, reports from the Iranian capital said yesterday.

The Glasgow Herald, *10 March 1986*

1. An Evening in Town (see page 21).

   These pictures summarise aspects of events which took place when four friends went out one evening. Write down brief answers to the following questions:

   **(a)** How are violence, aggression and conflict involved in this story?

   **(b)** How do you know that John was both verbally and physically aggressive?

   **(c)** Give two examples of how John was involved in anti-social behaviour.

   **(d)** What punishment do you think the magistrate might have imposed on John after he was caught?

   **(e)** Do you think John's parents might be at fault? Say why.

   **(f)** Imagine that you are John's father. What would you say to John when you first heard that he was to appear before a magistrate for committing an offence?

2. Put each of the eight press headings on page 23 under one of the following forms of violence:   **(a)** direct   **(b)** structural   **(c)** mental   **(d)** environmental.

3. In the cartoon on page 22, why do you think the child is about to throw a brick?

4. **(a)** Select three of the list below which, in your opinion, are most likely to contribute to the following:

   **(i)** petty theft, such as shoplifting by a 16-year-old

   **(ii)** vandalism or assault by a gang or 'firm' of young football hooligans

   **(iii)** drug-trafficking by a professional gang

   **(iv)** fraud by business 'wheeler-dealers'

   **(v)** riots in an inner city area by youths aged 16–30

   **(vi)** child or wife battering by a father.

   **(b)** Which three items in the list below do you think are particularly important in terms of causing the following:

   **(i)** stress

   **(ii)** verbal aggressiveness or yobbish behaviour?

       Lack of proper parental guidance or control

       Lack of discipline at school

       Unsuitable school curriculum

       Ill-treatment at home

       Too much work/responsibility

       Lack of self-discipline

       Lack of religious/moral values

       Past leniency in dealing with past offenders by judges/magistrates

       'Opportunism', that is acting on the spur of the moment as the opportunity arises

Difficulties in making friends with the opposite sex

Boredom and need for excitement

Poverty or unemployment

Government policies and laws

Influence of the mass media, comics, toys, 'video nasties', war games, etc.

Poor housing

Excessive noise

Police provocation

Form of bravado to please group and not to be thought of as a coward

Earning a living

Money problems or need for extra earnings

Bad weather or natural disasters

Racial discrimination

Loneliness and few friends

5.  Class/group project.
The class could be divided into small groups of about four. Each small group could collect material relating to each of the topics below, explaining how each extract they collect illustrates an aspect of conflict (types, origins, solutions, coping, etc.). Afterwards group reports, class discussion or perhaps an exhibition of material can be arranged. Alternatively the whole class could pick only one of the topics and choose others later when more chapters of the book have been studied.

(a) the family in various novels, using sources such as *Kes* or *Joby*

(b) jokes and cartoons

(c) advertising and posters

(d) television plays, serials or situation comedies

(e) films

(f) photographs and paintings

(g) quotations, proverbs, parables and fables.

# 2 CONFLICT AT WORK OR IN BUSINESS LIFE

## Introduction

Competition is a key concept in business. Rivalry is common between firms selling similar products, who may advertise and change prices to try to increase sales. However, conflicts of interest (2 and 3 below) or conflicts of value (1 below) play an important part in economic and industrial life. Points 1 and 2 are covered in more detail in this chapter. These two forms of conflict were explained in Chapter 1.

**1.** Opposing economic beliefs and systems (see the ideas of Adam Smith and Karl Marx, explained below. These ideas are at the root of the East–West ideological conflict, refer to page 90).

**2.** Opposing interests or divisions between bosses and workers or between management and employees.

**3.** Conflict of interest between producers and others, for example consumers. Producers often want to sell as many goods as possible at the highest possible price so as to make the most profit. In contrast, consumers want to buy the best goods at the lowest possible price.

---

Business is simply about winning battles in the market-place by outmanoeuvring an opponent to obtain a superior profit position.

*Barrie G James*, Business Wargames, *1985*

---

## Two Opposing Views of Economic Life

**Champion of private enterprise or capitalism: Adam Smith (1723–90)** This Scottish academic presented his views in a book called *The Wealth of Nations* which had a considerable influence on the growth of capitalism and on British government policies until about the mid-1850s. Only then did the government start to introduce extensive legislation to improve the social and economic conditions of workers. Smith argued that

**1.** An economy should regulate itself. Even though individuals act from self-interest, they are led by an 'invisible hand' towards the common good.

26

2.   The government should not intervene in the economy. If the government limited its role to that of keeping law and order, and to raising taxes to pay for necessary administration including the legal system, then each individual would be free to show initiative and enterprise.

**Champion of communism: Karl Marx (1818–83)**   Marx was a German philosopher. Some of his ideas were presented in a short work called *A Manifesto of the Communist Party* (1848) which he wrote with his friend Friedrich Engels. His views had an impact on the development of socialist parties in Europe, and particularly on the leaders of the Russian Revolution (1917) and the subsequent growth of communism. He argued that

1.   The interests of bosses and workers are inevitably opposed to one another. As society evolved from slavery to feudalism and then to capitalism, a struggle developed between two classes. Under capitalism these two classes took the form of a small group of owners of businesses and their paid representatives (directors or managers) who benefited from exploiting a much larger group of workers. If the workers received the full benefits of their work, that is the profit, then the capitalist would receive no profit and the system would collapse.

2.   Change can only come through revolution. Workers will only gain their freedom and just rewards if they unite in a communist revolution to overthrow the existing order.

# Two Approaches to Solving Disputes

**The win-lose approach**   In this view, life's struggles and disputes are seen as sports contests or gun fights when one side is expected to win and the other to lose, unless a draw results. This clash or confrontation approach reflects the way in which many in the West view political, economic and social issues. Many industrialists and workers see the business world like this, the belief being that there is only a limited amount of things to be shared, whether land, or markets or wealth. It is as if there were only one cake of a certain size, and each person can only increase his or her share at the expense of others. (Note the quote from James' book on page 26).

Adam Smith believed that competition between businesses under the conditions of private enterprise led to the greater benefit of all. Karl Marx lived later than Adam Smith and was able to see some of the drawbacks of unregulated capitalism. For example, under a win-lose approach two rivals may make deals to avoid their mutual destruction, or they may co-operate in business to share a market. This behaviour was one factor which led to the growth of large business and monopolies (a monopoly is a business which controls all the products or services in one industry, having eliminated all rivals).

By Workers' Toil Alone

TGWU Record (British)

T and G Record, *August 1979*

No man profiteth but by the loss of others.

*Michel de Montaigne 1533—92*

The worst crime against working people is a company which fails to operate at a profit.

*Samuel Gompers*

T and G Record, *March 1986*

**The mixed economy (the half-way house)**  Totally unplanned and totally planned economies both have their disadvantages. If little is regulated the poor and weak often suffer at the expense of the rich and powerful. If virtually everything is regulated, or there is little competition, the individual lacks any incentive to give his or her best. In the USSR the best results in agriculture have tended to come not from the large state-owned farms but from privately-owned plots, where farmers can sell their surplus crops. Practically all countries today are in various degrees 'mixed economies', where capitalism and socialism exist side by side and major sectors of the economy are partly privately and partly state-owned. The best examples of mixed economies are to be found in Western Europe.

**The co-operative approach or 'winners all'**  Numerous examples exist in life of how people co-operate so that things function properly in the interests of everyone, whether at home, at work or at leisure.

Workers form trade unions in order to gain strength through unity in their negotiations with their employers, particularly about wages and work conditions. Traditionally workers and employers have seen their interests as opposed. The employer tries to get as much work out of each employee for the least possible wage, while the worker tries to work as little as possible for the wage he is paid. Sometimes strikes by workers harm both sides. One solution is to allow some worker participation in the decisions that are made governing their lives, which in turn will help improve morale and output.

The idea is that the cake is not limited to any particular size, and that by co-operation the cake can be enlarged, so that everyone can gain, and not necessarily at the expense of each other. (See the extract by Harper.) Another example is where two governments or businesses agree to develop jointly or to share disputed resources, such as land or rights to fishing and mining.

---

## WHY WE GERMANS WIN

Of course, I can always do with more money. But we live well, and to strike for more jam would damage the company's ability to pay me more from better profits next year. It might even lose me the loaf.

*Stephen Harper*, Daily Express, *11 July 1974*

---

Opponents of the co-operative approach include the following: (a) pessimists who believe that wars, bitter conflicts and violence will always be with us; (b) idealists who believe that only through peaceful or violent change can conditions be brought about to ensure effective co-operation.

*A First World War munitions factory*

# Why People Work

People spend most of their time when awake at work, and so the workplace, whether a farm, office or factory, is a central and essential part of their lives. Work allows us to earn money to live and support our families. It also enables other basic human needs to be met, such as self-respect, acceptance and recognition by others, opportunities to make friends and to play a fuller part in a community. People do not want to be treated as slaves or to be exploited simply for the benefit of others. Efforts are often made to improve work conditions, and to treat workers not as mere cogs in a wheel but as people making a worthwhile contribution to the success of an enterprise, and who are entitled to participate in some form in making the rules which govern their work lives.

## THE YOUNG AND WORK

a) Many young people are unable to find work for lengthy periods.

b) Many young workers are unable to commence training in their fields of preference, in fact sometimes in any field.

c) Often young people are forced to accept positions as casual staff.

d) Even people able to find work are confronted with a whole new set of problems including:

- boring work
- menial tasks
- lack of responsibility
- health and safety problems
- inadequate training
- low wages.

*Position paper on Co-operatives, National Unemployment Congress of Young Christian Workers, Canberra, 21—4 August 1984*

## TREATING THE SYMPTOMS BUT NOT THE CAUSES

Once upon a time . . . a modern well-equipped factory was built in our town, creating lots of jobs. Despite good pay the work was boring and people got tired with the long hours. The machinery took little account of forgetfulness or ignorance and it was not long before workers received injuries. Soon an enterprising minister provided drinks and refreshments after work and a first-aid tent at the factory gate. One day someone died. Well-meaning religious people paid for his funeral and provided a large gravestone. Before long the tent grew into a fully equipped clinic and then into a hospital. But the injuries continued, and in spite of the hospital more and more people died from their injuries. Only then did people ask if it was enough to treat injuries, while leaving untouched the work conditions and machinery that caused them.

## ACTIVITIES

1. Define briefly the following words or terms: **(a)** casual staff **(b)** menial tasks **(c)** serfs. (See extract called 'The Young and Work', page 31.)

2. Why is work a central part of people's lives? Explain how the advantages of a job also illustrate some of the disadvantages of being unemployed.

3. What are the row of women making in the munitions factory shown in the photo taken during the First World War? (See page 30.) What injury or illness might the women acquire as a result of their work?

4. Suggest connections between the work conditions shown in the photograph and section (d) of the extract 'The Young and Work'.

5. Give examples of how the story 'Treating the Symptoms but not the Causes' relates to life in the early part of the Industrial Revolution in Britain. What legislation was passed by the government during the latter part of the nineteenth century to improve conditions of work?

6. Explain how the cartoon on trades union co-operation (page 29) illustrate the win-lose approach to resolving disputes.

7. How does the extract from 'Why We Germans Win . . .' (page 30) illustrate the co-operative approach to resolving disputes in a business?

8. The employer and the employee – a role play. Work in pairs. One person acts the role of the owner of a large, profitable private business and the other that of a trade unionist who is a member of a left-wing party. What might you say to each other about the strengths and weaknesses of the various forms of an economy (market, planned and mixed)?

# 3 LAW-MAKING, INTOLERANCE AND NATIONALISM

## Introduction

This chapter covers some of the reasons why we need laws and some of the problems which cause barriers and misunderstandings between people and between countries.

Section 3.1 looks at two main forms of decision-making which correspond roughly to the two main forms of government in the world, democratic and non-democratic. Sections 3.2 and 3.3 provide examples of prejudice and intolerance, showing that some views of people even in democracies may not be truly democratic.

## 3.1 Making Laws and Decisions

### Democratic and Non-democratic Government

A basic conflict occurs over how laws and decisions are made. In a democratic country all adult citizens (over 18 years in Britain) have the right to vote in free elections at regular intervals for a candidate to represent them in a parliament or assembly. The political party which obtains the most representatives forms the government and is then responsible for making and changing the laws. In Britain, the most important committee of the government is called the Cabinet, and this group (about 20–5 leading ministers appointed by the Prime Minister) is responsible for making important decisions.

There are various forms of non-democratic government, but basically they are led by one person or small group who have not been chosen by the citizens to represent them, and who retain absolute power through control of the armed forces, the police, the mass media and so on. Laws under such rule may be passed which do not benefit the people, who are powerless to change the government unless they risk trying to do so by force in a rebellion.

**Direct and indirect democracy**   The principles of democracy can be applied to any organisation or group. If the group is small, direct democracy is possible. All members can participate in making the decisions or rules which affect them. In a large organisation the members elect the representatives who will take the decisions for them. This is known as indirect, or representative, democracy and is the way government works in Britain.

**Examples of democracies**   Refer to the map on page 183 (Chapter 11). You will notice that only a small part of the world is actually described as 'free'. This part corresponds more or less to what people in Britain and the Western world understand by democratic government. The parts marked as 'partly free' or 'not free' are various forms of non-democratic government. Further details are provided below.

**Anarchy**   Refer to the illustration 'Why do we need laws?' on page 36. If laws and rules did not exist, most people think life would be confused and disordered – or anarchy. However, a very small minority of people in some countries argue that most laws and rules, and government itself, represent a form of oppression. Life would be freer and people would co-operate willingly in managing their own affairs if organised government and most laws did not exist. Anarchy does not occur anywhere as a form of rule for a country or large organisation, though its principles are applied to simple communal living of some small groups. Most people think that it would be impractical for any large group.

---

All power tends to corrupt and absolute power corrupts absolutely.

*Lord Acton*

---

**Limitations of democracy**   While democracy is regarded as the best form of rule because it allows the greatest freedom for individuals, there are times when decisions might be made autocratically, that is without reference to the people or their representatives, when special skills or knowledge are required, or a crisis occurs, and there is a need to save time and cost. In September 1939, for example, the British Parliament suspended democratic freedoms and rights when the government was granted emergency powers for the duration of the Second World War.

Democracy is considered more applicable to certain situations than others. For example confusion and chaos might result if a group of soldiers in training for battle, or the crew of a large plane, had the right to question every decision which was made by the person in charge. In fact under some circumstances an individual may make better or more sensible decisions than those of a group, since he is immune to being influenced by emotions and hysteria which can sometimes influence a group, or cause the individual to accept the decisions of a majority. Some of the drawbacks of group decision-making are mentioned on page 37.

We rule you

We fool you

We shoot you

We eat for you

We feed all

*A Marxist view of pre-revolutionary Russian society*

# Why do we need laws?

Imagine the local bully is allowed to run free . . .

Picking on individuals.

But if the individuals get together . . .

They can decide — no more bullying or else!

Now they have made a rule — and you can see that the rule will only be effective as long as they enforce it.

The same is true of the laws that govern society.

**Laws make up the framework of everyday life.**

**Laws protect us from others.**

If there were no traffic laws . . .

People would be able to drive on whichever side of the road they wanted (or on the pavement if it suited them). They would be allowed to go as fast as they liked, and park sideways across the street. No-one would have to pass a driving test.

If there were no laws about theft or violence . . .

Everyone would be free to help themselves to other people's property, being as brutal and vicious as they liked. Only those who could afford to arm themselves would be safe. But then, would the rest of us be safe from them?

If no-one had to pay taxes . . .

There would be no National Health Service, no free education, no Social Security or unemployment payments.

If there were no laws about employment . . .

Factory owners would be allowed to have workers using dangerous machinery in cold and leaky buildings. They would be able to sack people for supporting the wrong football team.

These are some examples of how laws affect the world we live in. Pick some laws and think about what would happen if we did not have them. How can they be enforced?

*CLASP (Crime, Law and Society Project), 1984*

# Differences between Individual and Group Behaviour

Often an individual thinks and acts quite differently as a member of a group or crowd than when alone. A person ceases to be calm and sensible under certain conditions of crisis or stress or when he loses his identity in a crowd. A person may become more emotional, or even hysterical, and feel less responsible for his acts. Out of a desire to conform or please, an individual may accept what the majority of a gang, team or crowd wants to do, even if contrary to his normal behaviour or beliefs. A person is more likely to agree with a group if the issues are not clear and if he has close contacts with group members over a period of time. However, an individual is less likely to agree if he is an independent thinker rather than a conformist.

---

## DESIRE TO GAIN ACCEPTANCE OR POPULARITY

A captain of a 707 Boeing on a flight from Tokyo to Hong Kong diverted the plane as his passengers wanted close-up photographs of Mount Fujiyama. The experienced pilot knew this was very risky as the clear blue skies above the mountain were the result of hurricane-force winds. The aircraft disintegrated in mid-air a few miles from the mountain.

---

## ACTIVITIES

1. Refer to the map on page 183. Which two of the following countries was not placed in the 'free category' by the US organisation, Freedom House? Can you think of any reason why this might be so?
   (a) Chile   (b) Botswana   (c) Bolivia   (d) Japan   (e) Nigeria   (f) Ghana
   (g) Austria   (h) Poland.

2. Look at the drawing showing a Marxist view of pre-revolutionary Russian society.
   (a) Identify or name the five groups described in the picture.
   (b) Find out two ways in which the bottom layer of Russian society was oppressed.
   (c) When did the proletarian revolution eventually occur?

3. Suggest four main ways in which a democracy differs from a non-democratic country. Refer to pages 180, 186 and 191.

4. Look at the diagram 'Why do we need laws?' on page 36.
   (a) Look at the picture on theft and violence. What view do you think the artist is portraying of human behaviour or human nature, optimistic or pessimistic? (Refer to pages 19–20, Chapter 1.)

**(b)** Look at the picture showing a factory boss. Discover four laws which have been passed since 1850 which still apply to safety and work conditions or to security of employment.

**(c)** Choose some laws and think about what would happen if we did not have them. How are these laws enforced?

5. Divide up into small groups. After preliminary discussion make a list of five possible conflicts involving a group as a whole versus its individual members. Then separately write down how you would react personally to group pressure under the five situations your group selected and the two below. Afterwards meet again as a group and compare results.

   **(a)** If all your friends smoked and you did not want to start, what would you do if they began to tease you?

   **(b)** Would you snatch a magazine in a local general store if your group of friends dared you to take one?

6. Discover the meanings of the 'pied-piper effect' and the 'band-wagon effect'. Explain how these ideas are linked to the influence of a group on individual behaviour.

7. Find out the answers to the following questions based on the Giles cartoon about Sir Oswald Mosley.

*The release of Sir Oswald Mosley in 1943 from imprisonment under Defence Regulation 18B*

(a) Who was Mosley and what political party did he lead before the Second World War?

(b) What does the symbol or insignia on his wings represent?

(c) Explain the significance of the sign he is making with his left hand.

(d) Why was he imprisoned?

(e) Defence Regulation 18B was one of the measures passed by Parliament when Britain when to war in 1939. Explain how this provides an example of the restriction of democratic rights during critical times.

8. The following represents a range of possible ways of making decisions for a group/club/unit/fighting force of 40 persons:

(a) Decisions are made by one person, possibly after advice from his or her own selected advisers.

(b) Decisions are made by one person after receiving advice from a committee elected by the group.

(c) Decisions are made by a committee elected by the group.

(d) Decisions are made by the whole group.

(e) Decisions are made by delegation of responsibility to individuals/pairs of individuals or small groups.

Imagine that the group is composed of adults or young people, single sex or mixed, according to the nature of the tasks below.

(i) Preparing an end-of-term play.

(ii) Christmas party at your house for guests of all ages.

(iii) Jazz or folk concert.

(iv) Hiking expedition for one day.

(v) How to spend the money of a school music club.

(vi) Defending a piece of territory in war against an enemy attack.

(vii) Mountain climbing expedition.

(viii) Organising a cooking roster in a week's camp and possibly the menu.

(ix) Selecting members of a team in a cricket club.

(x) running a Commune as an alternative form of organisation.

(xi) organising survival after being shipwrecked and stranded on a tropical desert island.

In small groups decide which of the alternatives (a)–(e) is the best way of making a decision for each of the situations (i)–(xi) above. State reasons for your choice. If necessary devise another method of decision-making.

Suggested references: William Golding, *Lord of the Flies*; George Orwell, *Animal Farm*.

# 3.2 Blind Spots, the Closed Mind and Propaganda

## Blind Spots

Each of us is liable to suffer at times from what are known as 'blind spots'. We see only part of the truth, or reinterpret information to support our own opinions. This happens particularly when we are on the defensive, or during a time of stress or crisis, or due to our personal loyalties (to family, friends or country), or our beliefs (religious or political).

During an emergency leaders tend to see a narrow range of options or available choices, as happened during the months preceding the First World War with the senior politicians and generals of the Triple Alliance and the Triple Entente.

**The distortion of reality**  The year-long miners' strike, led by Arthur Scargill, President of the National Union of Mineworkers, against the policies of the National Coal Board and the Conservative government, can be regarded as a crisis for those involved or closely affected. Pickets tried to stop miners breaking the strike by going to work, while police tried to make it possible for miners to go to work unmolested. Violence frequently occurred between police and miners. During the early months of the strike left-wing politicians who supported the strike tended to blame the police for the start of violence while government supporters tended to blame the pickets. A specific case of two conflicting versions of the truth during a time when emotions and feelings were running high occurred during the strike at the Orgreave coking plant. Note the following headline from the *Daily Mail*, and the details from the caption accompanying a photograph in *The Star* on 19 June 1984.

---

'Police hit me on the head' claims Scargill. *(The Star)*

'He fell . . . we were nowhere near him' say the police. *(Daily Mail)*

---

## The Closed Mind

Ideally, education should help us to develop an open mind and to be aware of new and creative ideas so that we will make our own wise decisions on certain problems and play an active part in a democracy. Some people, as a result of their own upbringing or experiences, develop warped or distorted minds and nurse bitter prejudices or hatreds. Their minds remain closed to any version of reality except their own. While it is best to develop an open mind and qualities such as tolerance, too much open-mindedness might lead to someone having no firm views of his or her own, or to an 'empty mind' (see Chapter 7). Probably most of us fall somewhere near the middle of a

# Scargill is injured in battle of Orgreave

• DAZED with pain, Arthur Scargill is lifted from the ground by helmeted ambulance men. The miners' leader was injured as 7000 pickets clashed with 3000 police and turned the Orgreave coking plant into the bloodiest battle field of the pit strike.

• Mr Scargill, who was detained in hospital overnight, claimed he was felled by a blow on the head from a police riot shield. The police say he slipped and hit a railway sleeper.

Picture: N. Pyne

The Star, *19 June 1984*

possible spectrum, tending to be narrow-minded on some things and open-minded on others.

## Characteristics of closed-mindedness

**1.** 'Black and white' (bipolar thinking). This is the view that there are only two sides to most problems. The closed-minded person thinks he or she is right in holding one view, the other view being the wrong one.

**2.** Ignoring contradictory information. Someone may have strong views on something on which he is ill-informed, and avoids people or reading publications likely to present views which differ.

**3.** Using techniques to support ideas. Unfair comparisons are made or appeals to authority, for example 'everyone knows that' or 'the newspaper says'. The person fails to listen properly to the views of others and fails to appreciate their feelings by making remarks such as: 'You need to have your head seen to if you believe that'.
The person is not willing to change his or her views easily or to admit error.

**4.** Inclined to be conformist or negative. The closed-minded person is inclined to be intolerant and prejudiced, discouraging new ideas with such remarks as 'that won't work' or 'that's silly'. He or she might want to cling to accepted practices, out of laziness, unwillingness to change, or lack of patience.

**Some examples of the closed mind**   In the 1900s a large manufacturer of carriage lamps for horse-drawn vehicles refused to make lamps for the newly invented cars. The owner insisted: 'these new-fangled contraptions are not here to stay'. The firm collapsed while a smaller firm which saw its opportunity flourished and expanded. This firm is today called Lucas Industries.

---

The aeroplane will never fly.                                       *Lord Haldane, 1907*

---

Bullets have little stopping power against the horse.                 *Earl Haig*

---

# Persuasive Language and Propaganda

Speakers and writers who wish to convince an audience or readership to support the activities of a particular group, a point of view, or policy tend to use persuasive words. Examples are advertisers, politicians and religious leaders. Journalists also use expressive or colourful language, especially in the headlines of the popular newspapers such as the *Daily Express*, *The Sun* and the *Daily Mirror*. The aim is to 'catch the eye' of the reader so as to increase sales.

# STANLEY  by Murray Ball

Continuing the adventures of the Great Palaeolithic Hero

Punch, *12 June 1974*

Three sensational or dramatic newspaper headlines

POLICE PUNCH GIANT HOLE IN BOMB RING

BL HOLDS FIRE IN CAR WAR

007 BEAUTY'S HORROR AS HOUNDS RIP UP CAT

## Propaganda

In the twentieth century the word 'propaganda' has come to mean the use of language and the manipulation of information and facts in such a way as to convince someone else that one side is right and the other side is wrong. It was used extensively in both the First and Second World Wars through posters, news broadcasts and the spoken and written word. During both World Wars the British and the Germans emphasised the victories and the good things they had achieved, and tended to minimise or ignore the defeats or bad things, so as to boost morale and their respective war efforts.

**'Nice' and 'nasty' words** An important aspect of propaganda is the attaching of pleasant adjectives to something you want people to support, and of unpleasant adjectives to something you want people to reject. Look at the cartoon below about the two missiles. Nice things are being said about the

Oliphant, copyright 1983 Universal Press Syndicate. Reprinted with permission. All rights reserved.

missile on the left and nasty things about the missile on the right. Note how Stanley in the *Punch* cartoon (page 43) is trying to make the snake seem small and a menace. He does not call him a 'freedom fighter', which some people think is a 'nice' thing to be called, but 'terrorist' and 'cold-blooded killer'.

**Euphemism** An example of the manipulation of language and distortion of words done by propagandists is the use of euphemisms. This is the use of pleasant words to describe something unpleasant. We all use euphemisms sometimes to avoid hurting someone's feelings. We might, for example, say that someone has 'passed away', rather than 'died'.

## ACTIVITIES

1. How can you tell from which countries the two missiles come in the *Guardian Weekly* cartoon on page 44?

2. Rearrange the following verbs in order starting with the one which conveys the 'nicest' meaning and ending with the one which has the most negative or unpleasant sound:
   massacre; obliterate; murder; kill; assassinate; execute; put to sleep.
   Look in a dictionary and distinguish clearly the meanings of 'kill' and 'murder'.

3. Find examples of militaristic or sensational words from the following:
   **(a)** the three headlines in this section
   **(b)** the headlines on page 23 in Chapter 1
   **(c)** two different daily newspapers during the last week. Concentrate particularly on the front and sports pages.

4. How are the following related: sport, nationalism, masculinity, militarism? Find examples from the press, books, posters.

## Pictures in the Mind

Most people put others into categories, classes or groups as soon as they meet, making estimates as to whether or not they are the sort of people they might want to make friends with. Based on often limited knowledge or first-hand experience, we also form views or opinions and mental pictures, or images, about people from other countries. These pictures may contain some truth and they may come close to reality if a person is well acquainted with the dress, food, hobbies, customs and lifestyle of others. There is a natural tendency to form impressions of others, but if a person is open-minded then he or she will be able to change his or her images or opinions as circumstances change or information becomes available which contradicts existing impressions.

Just as it is easy for a person to be biased or prejudiced in favour of a member of his or her own family involved in a dispute with an outsider, so it is easy for people to develop biases and prejudices against those whom appear completely different from themselves. If people hold opinions or mental pictures which are both inaccurate and unfavourable or negative, this can prevent or restrict the forging of better community, domestic or international relationships.

People are considered to be prone to prejudice if they make generalisations on the basis of limited experience, or if they base their views on no real evidence. For example, if a man has an unfortunate experience, such as being mugged by someone of a different ethnic or national group, he might assume that all people of that group behave in the same way.

## AN EXAMPLE: THE ENGLISH AND THE FRENCH

In 1969, *Punch* magazine polled both sides of the channel to find out what the French and English really thought of each other. The following were among the comments:

The English said that the French . . .
do not love animals, unless cooked . . .
drive their cars with deliberate intention to cause accidents . . .
only stop waving their arms to go to sleep . . .
have based the myth of their fighting forces entirely on Napoleon (a Corsican), lost all their battles since then and always called in the British to rescue them . . .

The French said that the English . . .
are arrogant (who else calls it the English Channel?) . . .
think they are still masters of the world, which is absurd; the top nation is, of course, France . . .
are calm at all times, not so much because of a stiff upper lip as an inability to become enthusiastic . . .
never talk in railway carriages, in the street or even at home – they only burst into speech when giving away confidential conversations . . .

ONE of America's proudest cities was under a state of martial law last night because of a family's refusal to bow to the brutal bullies of the Ku-Klux-Klan.

Carol Fox, from Banbury, Oxfordshire, and her black husband, Gerald, have been under siege since they moved into an exclusively white neighbourhood of Philadelphia a month ago.

But even in her worst nightmares Carol did not imagine that people could hate like this.

There are armed police in her front room and the white hoods of the Klan outside.

From BARBARA
JONES
in PHILADELPHIA

Christmas has become not a time for love and family happiness, but a battle to survive.

The first English settlers here called Philadelphia the City of Brotherly Love. Today a crowd stand outside the Fox home screaming: 'Move, niggers, move or we'll burn your house down.'

Mail on Sunday, *22 December 1985*

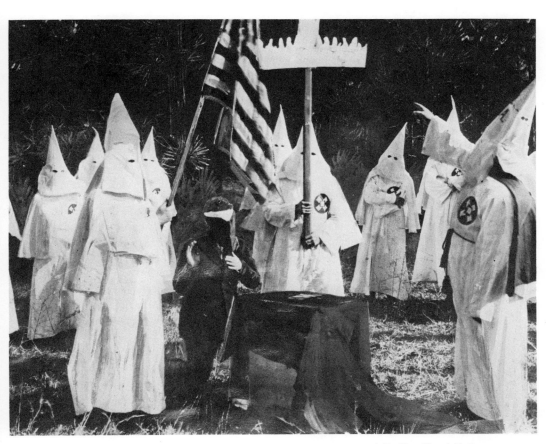

*A Ku Klux Klan initiations ceremony*

# FRANK CONVERSATION AT AN EMPTY TABLE

I suddenly caught sight of an empty table in the far corner of the room, empty inasmuch as three of the four chairs were unoccupied and the fourth was taken by someone who had hidden his face behind a newspaper. I threaded my way through the crowded room, guarding my precious cup of coffee from the noisy, gesticulating mob of boys and girls.

'Are these seats taken?' I asked as politely as I could.

The man lowered his newspaper for a second and replied with a gruff 'No.' He was a Negro.

I took my seat and began to sip my coffee in silence. Something about the man's attitude and the empty seats in a café with a queue waiting to find places made me uneasy—and curious. After a polite cough, I opened the conversation.

'Are you studying in Delhi University?'

The man lowered his newspaper again and replied as offensively as before. 'Yes, I am. Do you want to see my identity card?'

Before I could protest he had fished out his student's card and placed it on the table. He was from Ghana and as dark as they come. I put out my hand to him. 'I didn't mean to be rude: I just wanted to talk. I have never met anyone from Ghana before. My name is Singh. I am a professor at Aligarh.'

He took my hand gingerly and mumbled his name. My opening gambit was another faux pas. 'How do you like being in India?'

'Do you really want to know?' he asked, mincing every word. 'The truth, the whole truth, and not just propaganda!'

He told me of the few months he had been in Delhi of the hospitality extended by Indian boys and girls to 'white' (and occasionally 'brown') foreign students, but denied to Negro students; of the cold aloofness of the majority of Indians toward him and his fellow Africans; of the indifference of waiters in cafés to serve Negro patrons; of the crowded coffee house and empty seats around a table where a Negro happened to sit.

His words stung like slaps on the face. Weren't we the nation who more loudly than others proclaimed the equality of races and read holier-than-thou sermons to the South African whites and the Little Rock Americans?

'But our Government . . .' I protested.

'I said nothing against your Government,' he interrupted impatiently. 'It is your Government that has invited me and hundreds of other Africans to study in Indian universities. It gives us good scholarships . . .'

The Indian Constitution has abolished race and caste distinctions, but the Indian people are still a long way from abolishing prejudices based on race and color—for our caste system is essentially based on color complexes. The Sanskrit word for caste is Varna, which literally means 'color'. Varna goes back to the times when the fair-skinned Aryans invaded India over three thousand years ago. [There are five castes in India with Brahmans at the top and the so-called untouchables at the bottom.] To exploit the situation to their best advantage, the Aryans developed the caste system, based on occupation and the 'purity' of race.

On the top were the Brahmans, who had the monopoly of learning. Next came the Kshatryas, or the warriors, who defended the society. The third group were the Vaisyas, or the traders. The fourth were the Sudras, or the workers. And the fifth—the old aboriginal—was reduced to doing the most unpleasant jobs, such as scavenging and skinning dead animals, and was given no status in society by being declared an untouchable.

*Khushwant Singh*, UNESCO Courier, *October 1961*

# Feminism and Sexism

Women have often been exploited, discriminated against and treated unequally, rather like minorities in a society. Early efforts of women to acquire equal rights in Britain date back to the time of the suffragettes who campaigned before the First World War to secure the right to vote in elections and to play an equal part with men in a democratic political system.

In many countries a woman's place is regarded as being in the home. Often women and men appear more different from each other than they really are because they have been brought up and educated from an early age to do different things and expect different things. A child is expected to behave in a certain way according to his or her sex from the moment of birth. Thus a boy is expected to take an interest in toy soldiers and in physical activities, while a girl is expected to be interested in dolls and in domestic pursuits such as sewing and cooking.

Sexism is discrimination based on gender, which generally relegates women to inferior status within a society. A sex stereotype is a fixed and over-simplified idea of the usual behaviour, abilities or aims of persons of one sex.

---

## RIGHTS OF WOMEN

A famous saying of the Prophet is 'Paradise is at the feet of mothers'.

'It is the generous (in character) who is good to women, and it is the wicked who insults them.'

According to Islamic Law, a woman's right to her money, real estate, or other properties is fully acknowledged. This right undergoes no change whether she is single or married. She retains her full rights to buy, sell, mortgage or lease any or all her properties.

With regard to the woman's right to seek employment, it should be stated first that Islam regards her role in society as a mother and a wife as the most sacred and essential one.

However, there is no decree in Islam which forbids woman from seeking employment whenever there is a necessity for it, especially in positions which fit her nature and in which society needs her most. Examples of these professions are nursing, teaching (especially for children), and medicine.

*Thomas Ballantine Irving, Khurshid Ahmad, Muhammad Manazir Ahsan,*
*The Qur'an — Basic Teachings*

---

# Religious Intolerance and Conflict

**Some past conflicts**  One justification or excuse for wars and fighting in the past has been the desire to extend the way of life, beliefs or culture of one country or region to others.

In the past 4000 years various religions have been founded by leaders including Jesus, Buddha, Lao-Tzu and Mohammed. While they tried to create a worldwide brotherhood, none of these religions were successful in obtaining universal allegiance. Opponents were treated with intolerance and labelled in various ways ('outcasts', 'untouchables', 'infidels', 'heathens' or 'heretics'). They were often considered as fair game to be humiliated or killed.

In the past there have been bitter wars between the followers of Christianity and Islam, for example the Crusades.

Within Christianity itself there have been many splits in the past. First a division took place between the Eastern Orthodox and the Catholic churches. Then during the Reformation a split occurred between the Protestants and Catholics.

During the Catholic–Protestant religious war (Thirty Years' War, 1618–48) about two-thirds of the population of Europe died in fighting or through famine or disease.

**Present-day religious problems**  A major difference of opinion exists both within the Christian church and among Moslems between those who take a literal interpretation of the holy work (the Bible and the Koran), and those who take a broader view.

Among Protestants and Catholics there is also a dispute as to whether the main work of the church should be to save the souls of individuals or whether it should be involved in social and community work to help people lead a fuller life.

The two major Moslem groups are the Sunnis and the Shi'ites. Shi'ites take a literal or fundamentalist view of the Koran.

## ACTIVITIES

1. If someone asked you to give a 'stereotyped description' of the following, what would you say?
   (a) a secretary  (b) a doctor  (c) a dustman  (d) a politician.

2. Find out more details about the origin of the expression 'turning a blind eye' and its meaning. It probably originated at the Battle of Copenhagen (1798) when Horatio Nelson deliberately disobeyed the orders of his superiors by looking through his telescope with his blind eye so that he could not see the signals being relayed.

3. Many army leaders in countries such as Poland, France and Britain belittled the value of the tank in warfare at first out of loyalty to traditional methods of fighting based on the use of the horse. Find examples where army contingents made use of the horse in the early parts of the Second World War.

**4.** Answer the following questions based on the cartoon of a Frenchman on page 46.

**(a)** What is the Frenchman holding under his arm and what is in his pocket?

**(b)** Name the person he is thinking of.

**(c)** What is the Frenchman wearing on his head? What do you think the objects represent that look like bricks?

**(d)** Suggest reasons why this picture is a stereotype, not necessarily true of a typical Frenchman in 1969 or today.

**(e)** Some people from other countries used to think that the typical Englishman wore a bowler hat, a pinstripe suit and carried an umbrella. Of what sort of Englishman did this used to be true? Where would you still find people dressed this way today?

**5.** Under the influence of men such as Nehru and Gandhi the people considered to be without a caste, the 'untouchables', were called Harijans instead. Explain the origin and role of the caste system. Suggest reasons why it has been difficult to eliminate in India.

**6.** Explain how Singh's article describes the difficulty of enforcing laws regarding human and community relations. Suggest reasons for the persistence of barriers such as class, religion, nationality, ethnicity or race which divide people. How do you think such barriers can be overcome?

**7.** Find out the answer to the following questions on the Ku Klux Klan:

**(a)** For what reason was this organisation founded in the Southern States after the American Civil War?

**(b)** Why do you think its main support comes from blue-collar poor whites with few skills?

**8.** Discuss in groups the extent to which boys and girls are still expected to behave in a certain manner according to their sex.

**9.** Find out in what ways the Islamic view of the role of women was more progressive than the typical view in Britain until the 1960s or later.

**10.**    The Christian Church has a terrifying record in the persecution of both pagans and Jews (although it took over many pagan beliefs and despite the fact that Christ was a Jew).

(Adapted from George Mikes, *How to be God*, 1986)

Do a short research project and list some of the major criticisms which have been made about the practices of Christians and the Christian Church both today and in the past. Then in small groups take turns to present the criticisms and counter-arguments in defence of the Church. Refer to topics such as the following: wealth, the Inquisition, intolerance.

# 3.3  States, Nationalism and Patriotism

## Groupiness

Both animals and humans form groups. Humans, however, exaggerate the differences between themselves. These differences can be divided into the following:

- the outer marks, for example language, habits, clothes, sex, age, race or colour.
- the inner marks, for example religion, nationality, social class.

Naturally some of the outer marks such as clothes and behaviour may indicate some of the inner marks of difference. People tend to keep to groups familiar to them – 'birds of a feather flock together'. Whether out of ignorance or mistrust, a person might dislike or fear meeting strangers or those who are different.

**FURTHER ILLUSTRATION OF THE MINING DISTRICTS.**

*First Polite Native.* "WHO'S 'IM, BILL?"
*Second ditto.* "A STRANGER!"
*First ditto.* "'EAVE 'ARF A BRICK AT 'IM."

Punch, *1848*

It's great here in school, because all of us are as one, and nobody thinks about what different nationalities we all are. I am coloured, but nobody talks about it. Out of school, all of us get pressurised by our various ethnic groups to band together with them and not to mix with outsiders.

*Marlene Mangaroo, Liverpool 16-year-old schoolgirl*, Daily Mail, *28 September 1973*

# The growth of Nationalism

Where do you come from – which country? That's the question we ask first to pin down a stranger; belonging to a nation-state is one of our most important characteristics.

Yet the global patchwork of countries is of fairly recent origin – and nothing like as 'natural' a way of occupying the earth as you might think.

**A Nation** is a group of people who share a common history. They are likely to have the same culture and traditions and probably the same language.

**A State** is the supreme political authority within a sharply defined territory. But it is an abstract idea – since it is independent both of the ruler – who can be replaced – and of the subjects.

**A Nation-State** assumes that everyone within the territory of the state belongs to the same nation. The nation-state (loosely called a 'country') forms the basis of international political divisions.

**Nationalism** is the ideology which holds the nation and the state together. It takes many forms but usually involves a semi-mystical attachment to the 'historic homeland' and its supreme authority.

### Feudal Europe

The nation-state began to appear in its modern form with the collapse of feudalism in Europe. Countries in the Middle Ages tended to be run as the personal property of the monarch. The people were supposed to serve him and through him God.

53

### The French Revolution

The French Revolution of 1789 is generally seen as the turning point. With the downfall of the king, authority was now vested firmly in the new state. France was fortunate in having strong cultural ties between most of the people on her territory.

### The New Countries

After the Second World War intellectual leaders of many colonial territories pushed for independence. Steeped in the nationalism of their colonial masters, they demanded national liberation though in many of the new countries this meant convincing diverse groups of people that they all belong to 'one nation'.

### Nation-Building

To try and build one nation, traditional roots had to be rediscovered and embraced. This often resulted in a name change – from the Gold Coast to Ghana – or in choosing ancient cultures to identify with as in Zimbabwe. But the actual divisions are such that state rule in Africa nowadays often means rule by the dominant tribe.

### The National Security State

Where the rulers cannot hold their nation together by ideology they usually revert to force – in the 'national interest'. Latin American countries like Chile and Uruguay offer some of the most terrifying models of the 'national security state'. But the military coup is no surprise anywhere in the Third World.

New Internationalist, *May 1983*

## Nation-State versus the Multi-National State

The extracts from the *New Internationalist* illustrate firstly that the nation state is a comparatively modern idea, and secondly that it is not so easy to create a nation-state as one might imagine since people of many diverse origins and cultures may live together in the same territory.

In the past, attempts have been made to build new states out of former multi-national empires, as was the case following the collapse of the Ottoman and Habsburg Empires. The modern trend, however, is to try to create genuine multi-cultural or multi-national states. Most existing states contain two or more national or ethnic groups.

**Living together in a multi-national state**   Many countries have had problems in achieving racial harmony, partly because of intolerance and prejudice. In May 1966 Roy Jenkins, then British Home Secretary, said that he did not define integration, or the idea of diverse groups living together harmoniously, as assimilation. Assimilation is the way in which minorities get absorbed into the mainstream culture and lose their own individuality and culture. Rather, Jenkins defined integration as 'equal opportunity, accompanied by cultural diversity, in an atmosphere of mutual tolerance'.

# Dangers of Narrow Nationalism

**Narrow nationalism**   This tends to be associated with:

**1.** jingoism – the belief that one's country is never wrong

**2.** extreme groupiness or exclusiveness – the majority group may stress the need to defend its own culture and identity, which is associated with national identity, and fear that it might be swamped by others.

---

*EXTRACT FROM AN OPINION POLL CONDUCTED BY THE FRENCH NEWSPAPER, LE FIGARO, 10 DECEMBER 1985*

**Question** Among possible differences between the French and immigrants, is there one which makes cohabitation for you personally difficult to do?

**Answer:** Language 20   Religion 23   Colour of the skin 8
          Customs 49   None 27   No opinion 6

(The total of the percentages exceeds 100, since some of the people interviewed gave several answers.)

---

When I was about fourteen I had a lot of trouble because where we used to play football it was almost an everyday occurrence to be stopped with my friends and pushed against a wall and searched by about eight or nine policemen coming out of a black maria. They'd just come along, shove you against a wall, 'Come on lads, open out your pockets. What've you got?'

The Enemy Within, *Barbara Taylor*

---

Where do we stand now?
Our parentage pulls us one way
Our native land another.
Who do we fight for?
The West Indies? England? Britain?
Or the Atlantic Sea?

Stuck in a Futile Limbo,
With racism on one side
And misunderstanding on the other.

We are truly a Wandering Tribe!

*Julie Monica Plenty,* World Studies Journal, *Vol. 5 No. 3, 1985*

---

## INTELLIGENT PATRIOTISM

What I positively do not mean is that it is jingoism or nationalism that is a perversion of patriotism. . . . The other side of the coin of Gandhi's idea of religious tolerance is that peculiar form of madness we call religious bigotry – the obstinate and blind adherence to a creed that denies all merit in other beliefs. . . . World citizenship implies a sense of obligation to the people of other countries. . . . Charity begins at home but does not end there. Love of your own country is the secure base from which to reach out to others. . . . Unless we develop and encourage an intelligent patriotism of our own we shall not understand feelings of other peoples for their country and its culture.

*John Rae 'Why Patriotism is essential to World Peace', AGM of the Council for Education in World Citizenship*

---

What did you learn in school today, dear little boy of mine?
What did you learn in school today, dear little boy of mine?
I learned our government must be strong.
It's always right and never wrong.
Our leaders are the finest men
And we elect them again and again.
That's what I learned in school today
That's what I learned in school.

*Tom Paxton*

---

## ACTIVITIES

1.  In the cartoon on page 52 what inner and outer marks do you think distinguishes the man in a top hat from the other two men? Suggest an alternative caption for the cartoon.

2.  Look up the meaning of 'jingoism' and 'chauvinism'. Suggest a definition for 'narrow nationalism'.

3.  What sort of background do you think the children had in the extract from *The Enemy Within*?

4.  Explain how the extract by Marlene Mangaroo illustrates 'groupiness'.

5.  Study the results of the opinion poll published by *Le Figaro* on page 55. Discuss why the different customs of various groups of people can hinder their living together harmoniously in the same area. With reference to Chapters 7 and 8, suggest ways in which problems can be overcome.

# 4 NORTH–SOUTH RELATIONS AND ENVIRONMENTAL ISSUES

## 4.1 North–South Divisions

### Introduction

The first part of this section covers certain problems faced by the developing world and the way in which these problems are linked with the Western industrial world. The second part discusses the connection between possible remedies for the poverty of the developing world and world environmental problems including the shortage of energy.

### The Rich and Poor Worlds

The richest eighth of the world is mostly to be found in Western Europe, North America, and in Australia, New Zealand and South Africa (the white population) and Japan. The poorer countries of the developing world are mostly to be found in Latin America, Africa, the Middle East and Asia. Some countries are very poor partly because of very harsh climates and an insufficiency of basic resources to allow the people to be truly self-supporting. Examples are Chad and Mali (north-west Africa) and Bangladesh. However the wide disparity in wealth between the rich and poor countries can also partly be explained by the fact that rich countries, and the rich of the poor countries, have been consuming far more than their fair share of the world's dwindling resources. Six per cent of the world's population in the United States consumes nearly 50 per cent of the world's food supplies, while in 1984 the average American used 617 times the energy used by the average Ethiopian.

**The colonial period**   The former colonial powers, particularly Britain, France, Portugal and the Netherlands, must bear some of the blame for the problems of the developing world. During the colonial period colonies were largely exploited in the interests of the 'mother' country or colonial power.

## VITAL STATISTICS

| 1983<br>Country | GNP per head ($) | Infant mortality<br>(per 1000 live births) | Life expectancy<br>(years) |
|---|---|---|---|
| Bangladesh | 130 | 124 | 50 |
| Ethiopia | 110 | 172 | 43 |
| Burkina Faso | 160 | 176 | 45 |
| Sudan | 360 | 113 | 48 |
| Peru | 1000 | 95 | 59 |
| Ireland | 4970 | 10 | 73 |
| United Kingdom | 8570 | 10 | 74 |

*World Bank, World Development Report, 1986*

Little was done to industrialise the colonies or to provide many opportunities for education beyond the primary level. The colonies were expected to provide mainly agricultural goods and raw materials including minerals and to receive manufactured goods in return.

Transport communications were built not for purposes of developing the country but to enable the export and import of goods, notably in West Africa. The senior posts of responsibility in administration, health, education, industry, mining, and so on, were reserved for Europeans. Attempts to get non-white participation in politics were meagre before the Second World War as the colonial powers hoped that they would, in most cases, be able to retain their colonies indefinitely, with the Europeans holding political and economic power.

**External problems of new states after independence**    The developing countries won their freedom from colonial rule mostly in the 1960s, in some cases by violent struggle. However, as Dr Nkrumah, first leader of Ghana, and others have pointed out, many of the new states did not have real independence. Many decisions affecting their economies continued to be made by Western governments, or by multinational companies which dominated many key industries or agricultural products through the ownership of businesses and land. More recently some Third World governments have imposed controls on multinational businesses, and insisted that the local inhabitants should have a sizeable involvement in the ownership and management of a branch of a foreign business operating within their borders.

---

The corporations have no interest in producing goods suitable for the consumption or use of the poorest 60% of the population. They are not in the business of producing low-cost housing, cheap and nutritious food, or village medical care.

*R Barnet, 'Multinationals and Third World Development', Multinational Monitor, 1980*

## GUESS WHICH ONE HE WILL INVEST IN.

*F E Trainer*, Critical Social Issues — Topic 1, Limits to Growth, *1984*

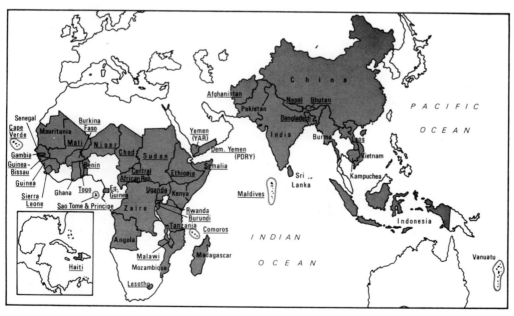

*Map of the world's poorest countries*

**The need for land reform in Latin America** Latin American countries won independence from Spain (or in the case of Brazil, from Portugal) mostly in the early 19th century. In this part of the developing world the United States has exercised powerful political and economic influence. In the developing world wealthy local élites and leaders often work hand in hand with foreign governments or businesses. For example, one need in Latin America is land reform, which includes the breaking up of large feudal estates, since about 93 per cent of the farmland is owned by about 7 per cent of the people. However, when a moderate government in Guatemala tried to nationalise unused land owned by the American United Fruit Company, the largest landowner, the overthrow of the government, supported by the Americans, prevented this. Some Latin American governments are military dictatorships which resist by force any attempts of the people to obtain reforms.

*Universal Press Syndicate, 1986*

**Problems in Nigeria after independence** Some of the developing countries after independence, despite many advantages, found it difficult to maintain political and economic stability. One example is Nigeria and the extract below summarises some of its difficulties.

Since the British flag was hauled down in 1960, this land has endured every evil which mankind is capable of inflicting on itself: not just corruption at every level of government, but a civil war of unimaginable savagery, incompetence on a truly criminal scale, one of the worst crime rates in the world and the systematic exploitation by successive rulers of their own people.

Small wonder if there is cynicism about the promises of General Buhari that he will put things right. For though military rule in Nigeria has generally proved to be better than civilian government, it has never come near solving the problems which are crippling Nigeria.

Yet this country could and should have become the showpiece of Africa.

It has some of the most resourceful and intelligent peoples in the whole continent. It is stuffed full of natural resources. It is capable not only of being self-sufficient in food but of being a big food exporter.

Above all it has huge deposits of oil, and as yet untapped reserves of natural gas. It is the world's eighth largest oil producer, and at one time was earning £10 000 000 a day in oil sales alone.

Yet the dream of a rich and powerful Nigeria began to go sour long ago.

After independence in 1960 the bitter tribal rivalries which had been disguised by British rule began to show themselves once more. . . . It required a bribe to get into the country and another bribe to get out. It required a bribe to build a house or sell a car or even to get a room at an hotel.

'The vast riches that brought only misery to Nigeria', Sunday Express, 8 July 1984

# Western Aid Policies

Western aid policies have sometimes aggravated the difficulties of the poorer states. When poor countries have been short of capital funds for development, aid from the West has taken the following forms:

**1.** free donations collected by charities such as Oxfam;

**2.** loans granted by governments and international agencies such as the World Bank or the International Monetary Fund, sometimes on favourable terms;

**3.** technical aid, training and advice provided by government, private or international agencies. Often aid given by governments was on the condition that the countries receiving the aid spent part of the funds on buying goods from the donor country. As a result of bureaucracy and corruption part of the funds raised by charity often did not go to the people most in need but into the pockets of unscrupulous middlemen.

**Aid for the Sahel drought**   The needs of subsistence farmers and the poor in the Sahel have often been neglected in aid programmes by both governments and aid donors. Newly independent countries often neglected agriculture and concentrated on efforts to industrialise and build ports, roads, railways and harbours. After the Sahel drought in 1968–73 some $7.7 billion was given in aid, but little of this went on agriculture. Efforts to improve agriculture concentrated on commercial 'cash' crops like cotton and groundnuts, which could be exported, rather than on domestic foods like sorghum and millet.

Development tends to be based on commercial rather than humanitarian interests.

**Developments in the Third World** Governments often followed policies based on commercial rather than humanitarian considerations. Aid and investment tended to be spent on areas which yielded the most profit (goods needed for export or bought by the rich) rather than on projects which helped the needy, as in the case of the Sahel discussed on page 61. Perhaps one-fifth of the soil of the developing world now grows things such as coffee, cocoa, tea, sugar and bananas. Local businessmen and landowners benefit while little of the wealth 'trickles down' to the poor.

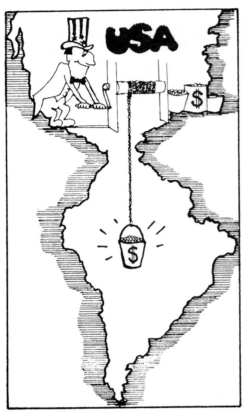

In the past American companies dominated key sectors of certain industries in Third World countries, as in the case of Cuba, where until 1959 half of the land was American-owned and the USA was the main market for Cuba's goods, especially sugar. American aid programmes have been criticised for (a) going mostly to pro-American governments; (b) mainly helping the local rich; (c) benefiting American companies involved in producing some of the exports from, or imports to, the Third World.

Resurgence, *Vol 4, No 6*

## Military Rule in the Third World

Internal divisions, economic problems, inexperience in government, are some of the reasons why many developing countries have had difficulty in maintaining stable democratic rule. Frequently democratic civilian rule has been replaced by military rule (as in Nigeria periodically) or by a dictator or family clique (as in Nicaragua from the 1930s until 1979). Often such rulers have maintained their power by increasing spending on arms imported from abroad rather than on improving the working and living conditions of their people. Western powers such as the USA, Britain and France have been prepared to supply arms since this represents profitable business and helps gain allies in the Cold War with the Soviet Union.

# ACTIVITIES

1. What example is given in the extract on Nigeria concerning corruption? Can you think of ways such corruption might have been avoided?

2. When another severe drought came to the Sahel 1983–5 explain why you think there was widespread famine despite the measures taken to deal with the previous drought. Find the Sahel region of Africa on a map. Name three countries in the Sahel.

3. Find out what is meant by the following: **(a)** the North **(b)** the South **(c)** the First World **(d)** the Second World **(e)** the Third World **(f)** the Fourth World **(g)** neo-colonialism.

4. Explain the significance of the table 'Vital Statistics' on page 58. What is meant by 'GNP per head ($)'? What do the three columns, looked at together, tell you about the lives of the people in each country listed?

5. What are the main regions and tribal groups in Nigeria? Give details of the causes and events of the Biafran War (1966–70). In what way were some foreign countries involved?

6. Explain how the three cartoons – 'Resurgence' on page 62, 'El Salvador' on page 60 and the one below – pinpoint problems of some Third World countries. Suggest how these problems are linked.

7. How did Bob Geldof help some of the drought-stricken countries in Africa during 1985?

8. Write a short essay commenting on the adequacy of the following comment as an explanation for the continued widening gap between the rich and poor countries.

> There is not much that we can do about the poverty of many developing countries as this is caused by the accidents of history, geography and climate.

9. Discuss in groups how relevant the following are to solving the present problems of three developing countries of your choice: **(a)** land reform **(b)** democratic rule **(c)** loans under generous conditions **(d)** irrigation **(e)** sanitation and health care **(f)** industrial development **(g)** reduction of population **(h)** efficient administration.

## 4.2 The Global Environment

The Club of Rome, a meeting of the richest, most influential countries, drew attention to the limited nature of the earth's resources in its 1972 report. E F Schumacher in his book *Small is Beautiful* (1973) talked about the world losing its natural capital, for example fossil fuels which cannot be recycled and 'living nature' such as the plankton of the oceans and the green surface of the earth, as a result of pollution.

Though the nuclear bomb poses the most immediate threat to humanity, in the long run the greatest threat may prove to be the peacetime peril of damage to the earth's natural resources as a result of human folly and greed.

All life on earth is dependent on the biosphere, the narrow layer of water, soil and air in which we live. Ronald Higgins in *The Seventh Enemy* (1978) lists six enemies as population explosion, food crisis, scarcity of resources, destruction of the environment, nuclear abuse and scientific technology. The seventh enemy is humanity itself – its blindness and apathy in the face of today's urgent problems.

Apathy and ignorance have made Man his own worst enemy.

We have stood by for too long, allowing commercial exploitation to pollute and destroy our natural world.

*Greenpeace advertisement, 1983*

How is pollution brought about?

There are seven main ways in which modern man pollutes and destroys the environment:

- By contaminating the atmosphere.
- By the indiscriminate use of pesticides.
- By radio-active materials.
- By contamination of water supplies.
- By dumping rubbish.
- By noise.
- By heat.

*Derek Heater*, World Studies

# Peace with Nature

West Europeans and Americans tend to define peace in terms of relationships among people. However, Africans, American Indians and members of some Asian religious groups also believe that relationships between people and the natural world are important. This is now echoed by modern scientists, conservationists and many non-experts. They all see war on nature, that is disregard for the environment and pollution of all types, such as the destruction of the natural habitat of many animals, as destructive to humanity itself.

**Economic growth versus conservation and protection of the environment** Most people in the West still have hopes of attaining even higher standards of living through economic growth. It is also argued that this is the best way of helping the developing countries since if the First World continues to prosper, there will be increased demand for the goods of the developing world, thus enabling the poorer countries to earn more from increased exports to pay for their own development and increase in living standards.

Another view is that the world's resources including energy are becoming more scarce and costlier all the time and will eventually run out. The rich states have exhausted many of their resources and rely on imports from the developing world for certain key minerals. (See Chapter 6, page 91.) It is not possible, according to this argument, for both the rich countries and the developing world to attain economic growth without causing damage to the environment as well as causing acute shortages of resources.

## The State of the Planet

Every year the world's deserts expand by another 80,000 square miles, every week 95,000 tonnes of sulphur dioxide are emitted in Britain alone, every day another animal or plant becomes extinct, and every minute 65 acres of tropical rain forest are felled.

A million people die of starvation each year, while 80 million people face the threat of severe food shortages caused by desertification in an area covering 20% of the Earth's surface. As the human population grows the strain on the land increases. In 20 years we will be sharing our planet's resources with 6 billion people . . .

Over the past twenty years the use of cars in Britain has quadrupled bringing with it a decline in the urban environment. Increased congestion, noise, stress, accidents and pollution are all too obvious. For those too young, too old or too poor to own a car the decline in public transport has restricted access to essential services, jobs and schools. The dominance of motor vehicles on our roads has meant that the bicycle has been pushed aside. A bicycle can travel 1,600 miles on the energy equivalent of one gallon of petrol, and unlike cars, is non-polluting, quiet, cheap and ideal for short journeys.

Mineral resources, built up over millions of years, are being wasted on over-packaging, non-returnable bottles and cans, and non-essentials. Even essential goods are designed to fall apart quickly or be 'disposable'. Huge amounts of our crucial energy resources are literally thrown away. In Britain only 70% of the energy used reaches the consumer. Electricity generation wastes 60% of the energy used, as steam is vented to the atmosphere instead of being harnessed to provide heating for homes, offices and factories.

These are just a few of the immense environmental problems facing Britain and the rest of the world today. If we continue abusing the resources of our planet we may one day find that it is no longer inhabitable. As Gandhi said, 'the earth has enough for every man's need, but not for every man's greed'.

*Friends of the Earth Trust*

---

One thing is clear: our brand of industrial and economic growth must end fairly soon. The most alarming thing about Spaceship Earth is the widening gap between the rich passengers and those living and partly living below decks.

*Gerald Leach, 'The Crisis to end all crises — Spaceship Earth', The Observer, August 1971*

*Tell me again how it was back in 1977 before we ran out of everything*
Time Magazine, *May 23, 1977*

---

*SURVIVAL 2000*

Fact 1.  Vegetation supports all life on earth. Without it all life would cease.

Fact 2.  As the human population rapidly rises the point has been reached where vegetation is being used faster than it is growing.

Fact 3.  Increasing world industrialization is increasing the destruction of vegetation through the manufacture of throwaway goods and pollution.

Fact 4.  Only 11% of the earth's land area is suitable for prime agriculture. Most of that is already under cultivation and up to 17 million acres of cropland is permanently lost every year — 125 000 acres in Britain.

*Friends of the Earth newspaper, Summer 1985*

---

**The forests are dying**  In West Germany experts say that about one-third of the trees there have died and that half of those left may be dying. Exhaust from cars is one of the causes, since trees lining the motorways are in particularly poor condition. However, many damaged trees have been found high up in remote parts of the forest. The precise link between man-made pollutants, acid rain and damage to the environment is not yet clear, but most agree that a connection exists. Industrial pollution may not

67

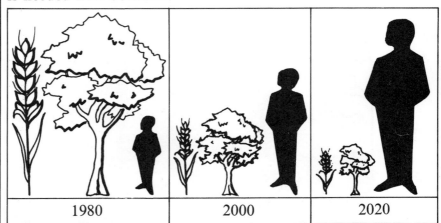

## Why a world conservation strategy is needed

A world strategy for the conservation of Earth's living resources is needed now because:

| 1980 | 2000 | 2020 |

If current rates of land destruction continue, close to one third of the world's arable land (symbolized by the stalk of grain) will be destroyed in the next 20 years. Similarly, by the end of this century (at present rates of clearance), the remaining area of unlogged productive tropical forest will be halved. During this period the world population is expected to increase by almost half from just over 4,000 million to just under 6,000 million.

Conservation Strategy, *International Union for the Conservation of Nature, March 1980*

be the sole cause since some experts argue that bacteria or other natural causes are destroying the trees. Other countries in Europe are also affected, especially the Scandinavian countries where damage is caused by pollution carried by the wind.

Trees are vital for a healthy world since they filter out pollutants and manufacture fresh oxygen. This is why air is far fresher in a forest than in an urban or industrial centre.

**The tropical forests in particular**   The rapid destruction of the world's tropical rain forests is one of the most serious environmental threats facing humanity. The causes of tropical deforestation are rooted in poverty. High population growth and shortage of land has forced millions of the desperately poor to the rain forests in search of food and fuel. Lacking proper skills and equipment to use the forest wisely, they burn ever larger areas for agriculture, which soon become arid and useless.

Rich farmers have done the same thing on a larger scale in Central America and the Brazilian Amazon region for cattle ranching so as to provide beef for hamburgers, hot dogs and pet food, mostly for US companies.

By the year 2000 about one-quarter of the world's wildlife will have been destroyed. Yet already half the medicines in the world's pharmacies come at least partly from rain forest products, and new sources of drugs are being discovered all the time from these. The disappearance of the forests leads to the extinction of ethnic groups of people. Over six million Brazilian Indians lived in Brazil when the Europeans first arrived, whereas now there are only 200 000.

---

When the forests go, rainfall drops, and fresh water supplies are disrupted. Even worse, their disappearance adds to the 'greenhouse effect' which most scientists expect will change the world's climate in the next century. One result could be that the Soviet Union rather than the United States becomes the world's leading grain producer, with enormous geopolitical consequences.

*Geoffrey Lean, 'Death of a life-cycle', The Observer, 24 October 1982*

---

One Sunday edition of the *New York Times* uses 150 acres of forest land.

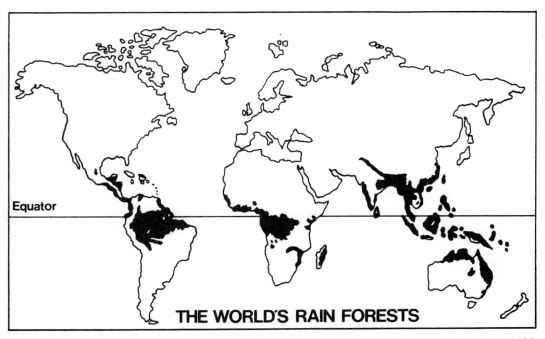

**THE WORLD'S RAIN FORESTS**

*Charles Secrett, Friends of the Earth, June 1985*

# ACTIVITIES

1.  What is the link between Ronald Higgins' book *The Seventh Enemy* (see page 64) and the extract on the same page from the advertisement by Greenpeace called 'Public Enemy No 1'?

2.  How is the idea of being at 'peace with nature' linked with one of the seven enemies of humanity mentioned by Ronald Higgins?

3.  Discover from the map on page 69 in which main countries the tropical rain forests are located. Mention two causes of deforestation.

4.  How is Gerald Leach's article on 'Spaceship Earth' (on page 66) linked to the material in the early part of Chapter 12?

5.  Explain how going to work or school on a bicycle instead of by car or bus helps to preserve the environment.

6.  What is the link between  (a) the consumption of hamburgers in the West, and the use of paper for writing, wrapping materials, etc, on the one hand, and (b) the world's forests on the other?

7.  Explain the relationship between problems of the pressure of population, the need for food and conservation of the environment.

8.  Give examples of how each of the seven main ways mentioned by Derek Heater (on page 65) help to destroy the environment.

9.  Discuss in a group practical ways in which you might help protect your local environment. If necessary write for details to Friends of the Earth. This organisation will also provide details of the World Wildlife Fund and Earthlife.

10. Discuss as a whole group Gandhi's comment 'the earth has enough for every man's need, but not for every man's greed' and its relevance to world problems. (Refer to Chapter 12.)

11. What does 'economic growth' mean? Suggest reasons why most countries in the world want to achieve higher growth rates, and why some people and organisations oppose this aim.

12. Find material from relevant sources to enable you to link up (or adequately explain) the following ideas in a short essay: rainforest; 'water cycle'; deforestation; less oxygen; more carbon dioxide, loss of the top soil; 'greenhouse effect'; possible melting of the polar ice.

*The United Nations Secretary-General, Pérez de Cuellar, visits victims of the drought in Ethiopia in 1984*

# 5 WAR

## 5.1 The Causes of War and the Justification of Violence

### General as Distinct from Specific Causes

Historians tend to study the *specific* causes of particular wars, such as the two world wars in the 20th century. This chapter is concerned with the *general* causes which explain why fighting and most wars take place. The three Ps – power, prestige and profit (economic gain or wealth) – can easily be remembered as important influences for many violent struggles in the world.

War would not occur if people were not willing or prepared to fight, and to believe or at least accept war propaganda (see page 78) portraying their side as being right and their opponents as being wrong.

Revolts are a kind of violence which may lead to war in certain circumstances. Two types of revolt are the following:
1. peaceful, as in the movement against the British led by Gandhi in India. (See page 120.)
2. non-peaceful, using physical violence.

### Revolt against Tyranny and Unjust Rule

**Oppressive rule**   Many examples can be found from the past and present of people living under conditions of injustice, hardship, and brutal rule. They may be forced to submit to such conditions from fear of what the government or its representatives, for example police and soldiers, might do if they protest, especially if they depend on rich, possibly absentee landlords, for their livelihood or work.

Sometimes people have been prepared to submit to the rule of a strong leader, a dynamic, charismatic personality or demagogue, who makes many alluring promises but ends in bringing disaster upon the country, as in the case of Hitler with the Third Reich and Mussolini in Fascist Italy. Some leaders who have gained immense popularity achieved much that was good and worthwhile, as in the case of the reforms in France of Napoleon Bonaparte, and the campaign for independence led by Gandhi in India.

**Awareness that change is possible**  It has been said that revolution occurred in France in 1789 because the people were not so oppressed or ill-informed as those living in other parts of continental Europe and knew that life was freer in Britain.

In a non-democratic country it is difficult for the mass of a people to campaign lawfully in favour of reforms. If the minority with power is not prepared to make changes voluntarily, and the disaffected masses feel that peaceful changes will not succeed, they may resort to violence and they may succeed if they are able to combine together effectively.

In Latin America some well-known personalities, such as Archbishop Helder Camara in Brazil, have tried to make the people aware of the unjust society which oppresses them and to give them encouragement in their ability to work for a freer society.

**The right to rebel**  In 1690, John Locke argued that government existed to protect the individual and that people had the right to rebel if their government failed to do this. Thomas Jefferson, influenced by Locke's ideas, proclaimed in 1776 that governments get their powers from the people, and that when any government fails to comply with the wishes of its citizens the latter have the right to change the government, by force if necessary.

Men are always ready to be slaves.

## The 'Just War' Theory

The idea of the 'just war' existed before the Christian era, but it became acceptable to Christians from the time of St Augustine in the fourth century AD, and was supported by the majority of Christians until the nuclear age. War is justified war under certain conditions. These can be summarised under three main points which cover the start, the conduct and the ending of a war.

**1.** The cause has to be righteous, defensive, aiming to secure justice while protecting the innocent. Its supporters should harbour no feelings of animosity or thirst for revenge, while reconciliation is the ultimate aim. It must only be undertaken as a last resort, following an ultimatum and a formal declaration of war.

**2.** The means must be controlled. The aim should be to inflict the minimum of violence on the enemy, and the gains should outweigh any losses.

**3.** The outcome or end must be predictable, that is there must be good prospects of a victory.

The 'just war' theory is not accepted by pacifists and the enormous power of nuclear weapons has led many non-pacifist Christians to wonder if war can ever be justified according to the three above points.

## ═══ ACTIVITIES ═══

**1.** Look up the meaning of the following words: **(a)** demagogue **(b)** charisma. Can you think of a 'demagogue' in history? Give an example of a 'charismatic' leader.

**2.** Study some of the past revolts which have taken place and suggest reasons why some have been violent and others have been relatively peaceful. In particular consider the following:

**(a)** opposition to James II of England

**(b)** independence movement in India

**(c)** opposition to the Russian Tsar up to 1917

**(d)** opposition to the Bourbon monarchy in 1830 in Paris.

3. Give details of the particular revolts that Locke and Jefferson had in mind when they were defending the right of rebellion. Why do you think they considered it acceptable to rebel in these instances?

4. Identify and explain the link between the observation by Tiberius and the cartoon 'Fighting for Freedom'.

5. Suggest a link between the King in Jesus' parable who 'counted the cost' before going to war (Luke 14 : 31–2) and the 'just war' doctrine.

6.

| Britain and Europe | Elsewhere or worldwide |
|---|---|
| The Crusades | Wars of the Spanish Conquistadores against |
| The Thirty Years' War | the Incas in South America |
| War of the Roses | Indian Wars in the United States |
| The Seven Years' War | War of Independence (American Revolution) |
| The Napoleonic Wars | Crimean War |
| Franco–Prussian War | Boer War |
| | First World War |
| | Italian–Abyssinian War |
| | Second World War |
| | Three Arab–Israeli Wars |
| | Franco–Algerian War |
| | Iran–Iraq or Gulf War |

(a) Which of the above had religion as a factor, if not the main cause, for the war?

(b) Which of the above were primarily dynastic struggles?

(c) Which of the above was fought exclusively in England?

(d) In which of the above was nationalism an important cause?

(e) Which of the above can be regarded as partly colonial or empire-building conflicts?

(f) In which one of the above wars was gas first used as a weapon?

(g) In which of the above did rival coalitions or alliances play an important part in causing the war?

(h) Which of the above could also be described as partly wars of genocide?

(i) During which one of the above conflicts was a team of nurses first employed to help the wounded?

(j) During which one of the above was the concentration camp idea first used?

(k) Which of the above were anti-colonial or liberation struggles?

## 5.2 Why People are Willing to Fight and the Role of Armed Forces

High morale means that every individual in a group will work – or fight – and, if needed, will give his last ounce of effort in its service.

*Field-Marshal Slim*

People are willing to fight for the following reasons:

**1.** To escape poverty, unemployment and starvation at home. In other words dissatisfaction or frustration with ordinary living conditions.

**2.** To have a regular organised routine, where everything is provided – food, shelter, companionship, regular employment and opportunities for promotion.

**3.** For adventure, excitement, the prospects of travel and escape from boredom and monotony.

**4.** To defend one's country and to do one's honourable and patriotic duty as a citizen.

**5.** Out of compulsion, since the alternative might be disgrace, imprisonment or sentence of death as a traitor.

Graffiti took the form of an additional important word on the publicity poster below.

A paratroop lieutenant has described the reason why a large number of young British officers joined the army. 'Oh, too many war comics, the idea of running around with a sub-machine gun and rather relishing the idea of being shot at . . . It's a pity to have gone through life without ever having done anything more dangerous than crossing the road.'

*Martin Woolacott, 'Changing the Guard'* The Guardian, *10 July 1973*

Take up our quarrel with the foe:
To you from failing hands we throw
The torch; be yours to hold it high.
If you break faith with us who die
We shall not sleep, though poppies grow
  In Flanders Fields

*John McCrae, 'In Flanders Fields', John Silkin (Ed.),*
The Penguin Book of First World War Poetry, *1970*

'On the Warpath'

War has been justified for such reasons as:

**1.** it helps to develop manly qualities – self-sacrifice, unselfishness, gallantry and bravery – and to develop patriotism and physical fitness.

**2.** it helps to unite a people – combatants and non-combatants – behind a common goal, to provide a sense of purpose and commit people to a definite cause.

Geoffrey Leon of *The Observer* referred to the Gurkhas as the 'finest soldiers on earth', in his article 'From Nepal to the Palace'

Among the many legends that surround them is the story of a paratroop regiment in the Second World War. The leader of the regiment asked for volunteers for a particularly dangerous drop behind enemy lines. About half the Gurkhas promptly stepped forward. The leader then went through what the volunteers would be asked to do. Half-way into his explanation, a surprised voice piped up from the back: 'Oh, you mean we can use parachutes'. Every remaining Gurkha joined the volunteers!

Radio Times, *1–7 June 1985*

# War Propaganda

War propaganda has as one of its roles the dehumanising of the enemy and stirring the will to fight among the armed forces of a country. People can find it easier to kill others if they are taught or trained to picture them as not quite human, or as people who have committed dastardly deeds. For example the Germans were portrayed in 1914 as Huns who had committed such atrocities as the bayoneting of Belgian babies.

In the armed forces human contact between officers and men is limited to keep the divide between the leaders and the led. Fraternisation with the enemy is naturally discouraged. For example no repetition was allowed of the Christmas 1914 truce when soldiers of opposing armies sang together and exchanged gifts.

*First World War recruiting poster*

# The Role of Armed Forces

The main functions of armed forces are:

**Strategic**  The armed forces are maintained in case of need to attack one or more states, or to deter one or more states from attacking the homeland, or to defeat the enemy if it is not deterred.

**Maintaining law and order**  This involves helping the government, the police and emergency services (fire and ambulance) in case of disaster, emergency relief, civil unrest, and subversive or large-scale criminal acts. The foreign aspect of this role includes duties in support of the United Nations.

**Ceremonial**  This applies particularly to armies. Even the Vatican City has an armed force of 220 Swiss guards.

**Foreign policy and diplomatic**  The basic aims of states could be summarised as survival, security, power, prosperity, freedom and peace. Armed forces reinforce a country's foreign policy in such areas as:

**1.**  Developing friends and allies, and joining defensive treaty organisations such as Nato.

**2.**  Having the armed power to influence events in the world.

**3.**  Maintaining national pride and self-confidence.

## ACTIVITIES

1.  How do you know from the cartoon 'On the Warpath' that it is a fight between British and German troops? Which are the British troops? In which war would this have taken place?

2.  What was one of the nicknames given by the British to German troops during the First World War? Illustrate why this was an example of the attempt to dehumanise an enemy.

3.  Which one (or more) of the functions of armed forces would soldiers be performing if stationed in the following places:  **(a)** on patrol in Northern Ireland;  **(b)** on guard outside Buckingham Palace;  **(c)** in barracks in West Germany?

4.  Give one reason why the war poster 'Your Country Needs You' would probably have been publicised during the early part of the First World War.

5.  Look up the definition of militarism. In groups of four list six ways children in general, and boys in particular, are subjected to military influence or the glorification of war in ordinary life.

6. In a group discuss to what extent, and in what way, any of the following are militaristic: (a) wearing of uniforms (b) brass bands (c) fitness training (d) game of space invaders (e) war toys or comics.

7. In what way could the following be said to exalt militarism (a) the story about the Gurkhas (b) the verse of a poem by John McCrae?

8. Discuss in a group some of the important factors which contribute to high morale among a fighting force. Would those factors vary according to the nature of the war?

9. Add three other reasons why war has been justified or defended as a legitimate measure.

10. Explain why John McCrae should refer to the following in the verse from *In Flanders Fields*: (a) Flanders (b) poppies (c) a torch.

*'Can't you guys get through to Gorbachev — at this rate we'll all be out of a job'*, Daily Mirror, *16 April 1987*

# 5.3   The Changing Nature and Types of Warfare

## Early Conflicts

War, organized war, is not a human instinct. It is a highly planned and co-operative form of theft. And that form of theft began ten thousand years ago when the harvesters of wheat accumulated a surplus, and the nomads rose out of the desert to rob them of what they themselves could not provide.

*Jacob Bronowski*, The Ascent of Man

When the first prehistoric tribe discovered that organization and weapons could eliminate danger from rival tribes – that, surely, was when war was born.

*Richard Humble*, Warfare in the Ancient World, *1980*

*'It was going to be the ultimate weapon, but I can't lift it'.*

New Internationalist, *March 1981*

## Conventional War

Most fighting now takes place between trained regular armed forces. This denotes all types of warfare used in the past and modern wars which do not involve the use of nuclear or chemical weapons. Before the rise of modern states, for the most part, fighting took place between trained private armies and hired mercenaries, while the civilians were not directly involved. This situation changed during the First and Second World Wars as civilians became involved in work connected with the war effort or suffered casualties as a result of aircraft bomb attacks.

Early man made use of weapons such as sticks and stones (including slings, catapults), then the bow and arrow and the sword. Later in the Middle Ages guns came into use (muskets and individual pistols), and artillery became more sophisticated from the time of gunpowder. The machine gun, invented in the 1860s, gave defending forces considerable superiority over attacking forces, and contributed to European victories over overwhelming numbers in colonial wars in the late 19th century. It was also a key defensive weapon in the First World War until the use of the tank enabled attacking forces to break the deadlock of trench warfare.

## Guerrilla or Irregular Warfare

Guerrillas wear no regular uniform and employ no normal military tactics. Normally guerrilla forces only attack government or armed enemies, usually have much popular support or sympathy, and confine their operations to one country. As their opponents are often more numerous and better equipped, guerrillas try to avoid large-scale pitched battles. Instead they make clever use of camouflage, trees and mountainous terrain or urban landscape, as a means of launching surprise 'hit and run' attacks.

Irregular or unorthodox warfare was used by the Spanish against Napoleon's troops (1806–10), by the Americans against British troops in the War of Independence (1776–83), and by the Russian Cossacks to harrass and hasten the retreat of Napoleon's French Grand Army from Moscow (1812).

Modern commandos or counter-terrorist units such as the British SAS (Special Air Services) have used similar methods.

Often those involved have been driven to revolt through the experience of oppressive conditions and foreign rule, and are now determined to rule themselves, or to choose better leaders. Examples since 1945 include the various anti-colonial movements or liberation wars as in Algeria, Angola and Mozambique.

## Terrorism

This has become prevalent since the late 1960s, and employed as an alternative form of warfare to conventional fighting.

Terrorists are invariably young and operate on their own or in very small groups, taking orders from a central office often in another country. In addition to attacks on military or police targets, they try to frighten civilians, including tourists, as a means of getting governments and others to accept their demands. Examples are the planting of time bombs in busy centres, hijacking of aircraft, and kidnapping persons to exhort ransom money. Such sensational acts obtain widespread TV and press publicity for groups and movements such as the IRA in Northern Ireland, the Red Brigades in Italy, the Palestine Liberation Organisation, and Arabs supporting the pan-Arab policy of Libya's Colonel Gaddafi.

State terrorism is where repressive governments order their troops and police to resort to atrocities to intimidate a civilian population, especially if they are sheltering known opponents of the leadership, as occurred in Nazi Germany and, more recently, in El Salvador.

# ACTIVITIES

1.  Summarise under three headings the main differences between conventional war, guerrilla warfare and terrorism. Suggest why some terrorists may have less public support than guerrilla fighters.

2.  Find out details of the guerrilla leader Che Guevara (formerly second-in-command to Fidel Castro in Cuba). Give at least one reason why you think guerrilla warfare might succeed and why it might fail, bearing in mind what you have discovered.

3.  Discover why urban guerrilla warfare became important in countries such as Bolivia, Uruguay and Argentina from the late 1960s.

4.  Explain why some individuals and groups turn to violence rather than non-violence as a means of overthrowing oppression and tyrannical rule. Base your answer on the following:

    (a) the Algerian War of Independence

    (b) civil war in Rhodesia before it became independent as Zimbabwe (1980)

    (c) the struggles of Fidel Castro against Batista in Cuba

    (d) the troubles in Northern Ireland since 1969

    (e) Opposition to the Shah in Iran in 1978–9.

5.       It is essentially a problem affecting the free world, not the communist bloc . . .
         American targets overseas were involved in about 25 per cent of all terrorism. Of
         the 695 total (terrorist incidents in 1985), the vast majority took place in the
         Middle East (310), Europe (184), and Latin America (125).

    'Unmasking Terrorism', The Christian Science Monitor, Weekly International Edition, 21–7 June
                                                                                            1986

    Find out answers to the following based on the above extract:

    (a) Why were many terrorist targets American?

    (b) Why did most terrorist incidents occur in the Middle East?

    (c) How would you define the 'free world'. Why should terrorism be particularly a problem of the free world as opposed to the communist world? (Note that only four of the terrorist incidents in Europe in 1985 occurred in Eastern Europe.)

# Nuclear War

Nuclear war is different from conventional war in that:

**1.** It might start at any moment, whereas a conventional war usually involves a slow build-up and a mobilisation period.

**2.** It would be enormously more destructive than any previous war.

**3.** It might start by accident, miscalculation or malfunction.

**4.** It might be the result of an escalation process. Many of the conventional attacking weapons today may be of little use in a major war as a result of the increased efficiency of defensive weapons such as guided missiles which make tanks and surface ships vulnerable. The first step after 'normal' conventional weapons would be 'battlefield' nuclear weapons, then so-called 'medium range' nuclear weapons, then the use of intercontinental nuclear missiles by the superpowers.

DOT CHART

1 dot — represents the firepower contained in all the aerial bombing by the Allies in the Second World War, including the bombs dropped on Hiroshima and Nagasaki: 3 megatons (3 million tons TNT).

6 dots — represent the firepower contained in the nuclear missiles of one Trident submarine: 18 megatons — enough to destroy every major city in the northern hemisphere.

6000 dots — represent the explosive power in the arsenals of the superpowers: 18 000 megatons.

Beyond War, *Creative Initiative Foundation*

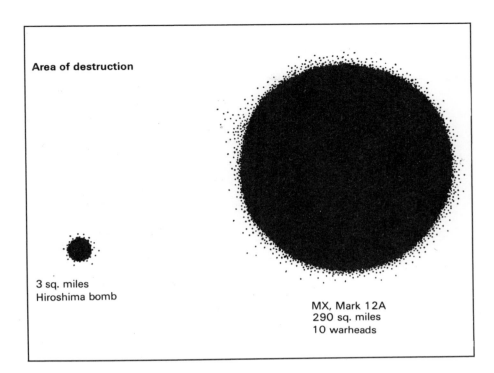

**Area of destruction**

3 sq. miles
Hiroshima bomb

MX, Mark 12A
290 sq. miles
10 warheads

## Chemical Warfare

Chemical weapons were first used during the First World War in 1915. These included phosgene and mustard gas whose smell gives warning for people to escape or to put on gas masks. Nerve gases are more popular as possible weapons since they are odourless and more toxic. Though banned by the Geneva Protocol (1926), several countries, including the USA, the USSR, and Britain, have reserved the right to use chemical weapons if other countries use them first.

## Biological Warfare

Biological weapons are living organisms or infective material derived from them which can cause disease or death in humans, animals or plants. The major countries are not keen to use this type of warfare since germs can spread rapidly, and being so contagious might be a military handicap if both sides suffered. This was one reason why biological weapons were banned in 1973.

## Non-ABC (Atomic, Biological or Chemical) Weapons

Modern technology has made possible various terrifying prospects for the future. Examples are (a) interference with the climate to produce artificial droughts or tidal waves and (b) hurricanes guided by the use of laser death-ray technology or robot warfare.

85

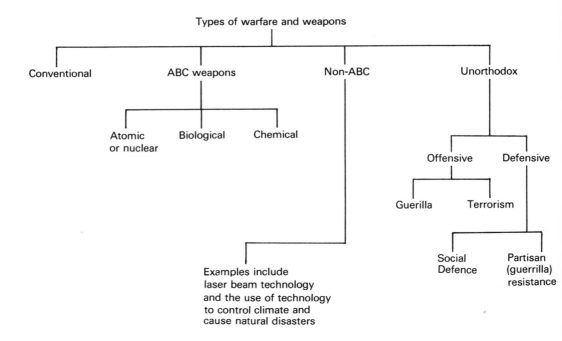

Types of warfare and weapons

Conventional — ABC weapons — Non-ABC — Unorthodox

ABC weapons: Atomic or nuclear, Biological, Chemical

Unorthodox: Offensive, Defensive

Offensive: Guerilla, Terrorism

Defensive: Social Defence, Partisan (guerrilla) resistance

Non-ABC: Examples include laser beam technology and the use of technology to control climate and cause natural disasters

## Alternative Defence

The failure of the superpowers to agree on measures for disarmament has led to a range of other possibilities being explored as an alternative to the other extreme of no defence at all against a foreign attack. Advocates of alternative defence to the use of nuclear weapons believe that it will make a nuclear attack less likely, with any potential aggressor resorting only to conventional warfare. In addition alternative defence is also envisaged in case a limited use of nuclear weapons resulted in the death of the political and military leadership of a country. The belief is that the civilian population should be trained in the art of military self-defence and survival.

**Five possible options are the following:**

**Conventional defence**  The armed forces are trained for defence purposes, the strategy adopted by Sweden. Use is made of defensive short-range weapons, that is those which can be used mainly inside one's own territory.

**Total defence or territorial defence**  The Swiss strategy is a variation of conventional defence. Instead of depending on defence by a small group of regular armed forces, reliance is put on support of 500000 troops (consisting of all males between 16 and 50 who have had to undergo periods of continuous military training) and 400000 civil defence volunteers made up of men aged 50 and above. The full-time Swiss army (with fewer than 2000 officers and non-commissioned officers) is a militia like the Israeli army. In the event of initial defeat and occupation, the remaining armed forces and civilians would conduct guerrilla struggle. Every male Swiss keeps a rifle while supplies of food, fuel and ammunition are dispersed throughout the Swiss Alps. Fall-out shelters, now compulsory for all new houses, could in theory protect over half the population.

**Partisan (guerrilla) resistance** This method involves abandoning conventional military defence with reliance put on prolonged paramilitary resistance to occupying enemy forces so as to make life as uncomfortable for them as possible. Examples were the activities of the Yugoslav partisans led by Tito against the Germans in the Second World War and the struggles of the Afghan rebels against Soviet troops in Afghanistan since 1979.

**Civilian non-violent resistance (social defence)** This option involves acts of non-co-operation such as strikes, boycotts, civil disobedience, mass demonstrations and various delaying tactics such as an industrial 'go slow'.

**Mixture of strategies** Civilian resistance could be combined with partisan tactics as employed in Norway during the Second World War against the Germans, or used as a last resort if other methods failed. The Swedes and Yugoslavs envisage a combination of conventional defence and partisan resistance, while a combination of these two plus social defence might provide an effective alternative model to the Swiss total defence strategy. Success would depend on units being small, dispersed, mobile, and autonomous and/or independent.

## ACTIVITIES

1. Which one of the following implies non-violent resistance to an aggressor:
   (a) partisan resistance  (b) territorial defence  (c) social defence
   (d) conventional defence? Can you think of good examples of two of these?

2. How is nuclear war different from conventional war?

3. From the list below identify four items which are used mainly for defensive purposes and four which are used mainly for offensive purposes. Which can be used for both purposes?

   (a) fort                       (g) mountain range
   (b) nuclear submarine          (h) an army
   (c) tank                       (i) aircraft carrier
   (d) helicopter                 (j) mine
   (e) napalm                     (k) anti-ballistic missile
   (f) cruise missile

4. Classify each of the following below (a) (b) (c) (d) under one of the following four headings:

ABC weapons
1 atomic   2 chemical   3 biological   4 non-ABC weapons

...............   ....................   ......................   .........................................

(a) robot warfare      (b) germ warfare

(c) nuclear warfare    (d) use of toxins (poisonous substances).

Is it possible to say which one of these would cause the greatest harm?

5. It might be hard to re-kindle in our armies today that spirit of high adventure in which they rallied to the colours in the old days.

*Major-General Sir John Marriott*

What do you think 'fighting spirit' means? What are the colours? Why might it be difficult to kindle the old spirit of high adventure today regarding army recruitment?

6. Dropping of the atomic bombs (1945) – some key dates:
6 August – a US bomber dropped an atom bomb, made of uranium, on Hiroshima, Japan.
8 August – the USSR declared war on Japan as agreed with the allies.
9 August – the US dropped a second atomic bomb (made of plutonium) on Nagasaki.
15 August – Japan surrendered.

(a) For what reasons do you think President Truman made the decision to drop   (i) the first and   (ii) the second atomic bomb?

(b) What decision would you have made in Truman's place? Would you have decided to drop one or two bombs, or would you have found another alternative?

(c) In the light of subsequent events, do you think Truman made the right decision?

(d) Imagine the type of advice Truman would have received from different sources before making any decision. List five points for and against the dropping of the first atomic bomb on Japan. What other alternatives might have been available?

(e) What link was there between the use of the bomb and   (i) Soviet entry into the war against Japan   (ii) the start and the growth of the Cold War?

7. Which of the three conditions and sub-conditions of a 'just war' could not be guaranteed if a nuclear war broke out? (See page 74.)

# 6 THE COLD WAR, ARMS RACE AND NUCLEAR WAR

## Introduction

This chapter gives the causes of the East–West tensions since 1945 as seen by Western governments and the majority in the West who largely blame the USSR for most of the problems connected with the arms race, the Cold War and the nuclear threat.

Almost all the points raised in this chapter relating to the Cold War and the nuclear threat can be used as part of the justification for rearming or for multilateral as opposed to unilateral disarmament. Put very simply, multilateral disarmament is where everyone disarms at the same time by mutual agreement; unilateral disarmament is where one country disarms irrespective of what other countries are doing.

The Guardian, *7 July 1984*

# 6.1 General Causes of the Cold War and Western Justification for its Defence Policies

## The Cold War: Definition and Scope

The Cold War came to reflect the course of East–West relations from 1945. Suspicion, general non-co-operation and intense rivalry characterised the relations between the Soviet Union and its allies, and the Western powers. The two new superpowers, the USA and the USSR, tried by all means short of actual war – for example propaganda, economic measures, aid to allies as in Vietnam – to get the better of the other.

**Causes of the start and continuation of the Cold War** Both sides are partly to blame. However a strong case can be made for the view that the East–West conflict was inevitable for reasons stated in **1.** and **2.** below. Some specific causes of the Cold War, as seen from American and Russian viewpoints, are outlined on pages 92–4 of this chapter and on page 142 of Chapter 9. Refer also to pages 26–7. The causes are:

**1.** Ideology. This is discussed in detail in Chapter 11, pages 185–7.

**2.** Big power rivalry. Even if the ideologies of the USA and the USSR had been similar, the Cold War conflict might still have occurred in terms of a struggle for world power and influence between these two countries which emerged from the Second World War as 'superpowers', more powerful now than countries such as Britain and France.

# Russia edges towards Vienna space talks

## By Jonathan Steele

The Soviet Union yesterday kept the door open for Soviet-American talks in September on banning the arms race in space, and urged the Reagan Administration to join a moratorium on the testing and deployment of all space weapons as soon as the talks begin.

3.  Economic rivalry. This is mainly reflected in the struggle for vital mineral resources. Some experts think that a major East–West war or serious confrontation could be caused by competition to obtain certain vital resources. The United States is now dependent on foreign supplies for 50 per cent of about 32 minerals considered vital to national survival, whether for industrial or military purposes. Most of such products are from the developing world, and some come particularly from South Africa and Namibia. (See table below.)

| Dependence of three NATO states on imported minerals | | | Dependence of four Warsaw Pact states on imported minerals | | | |
|---|---|---|---|---|---|---|
| Minerals | Federal Republic of Germany | United Kingdom | USA | Hungary | Poland | Romania | USSR |
| Manganese | 100 | 100 | 100 | 0 | 100 | 100 | 0 |
| Cobalt | 100 | 100 | 100 | 100 | 100 | 100 | 0 |
| Titanium | 100 | 100 | 55 | 100 | 100 | 100 | 0 |
| Chromium | 100 | 100 | 100 | 100 | 100 | 100 | 0 |
| Aluminium | 100 | 100 | 95 | 0 | 100 | 0 | 30–35 |
| Tantalum | 100 | 100 | 100 | 100 | 100 | 100 | 0 |
| Platinum metals | 100 | 100 | 100 | 100 | 100 | 100 | 0 |
| Tin | 100 | 85 | 99 | 100 | 100 | 100 | 25–30 |
| Nickel | 100 | 100 | 95 | 100 | 75 | 100 | 0 |
| Tungsten | 100 | 100 | 60 | 100 | 100 | 100 | 30–35 |
| Beryllium | 100 | 100 | 100 | 100 | 100 | 100 | 0 |
| Zirconium | 100 | 100 | 50 | 100 | 100 | 100 | 0 |
| Iron | 98 | 100 | 25 | 90 | 100 | 90 | 0 |
| Lead | 90 | 100 | 60 | 100 | 25–30 | 30 | 0 |
| Copper | 100 | 100 | 10–15 | 100 | 0 | 25–30 | 0 |

White Paper, Federal Minister of Defence, Bonn, 1983

Unlike the United States and Western Europe, the Soviet Union does not need to import most of these products due to its own substantial deposits of natural resources. The USSR is the second largest source of chromium and platinum group metals. Its industry is much less sensitive than the West to crises in the developing world.

The West interprets the interest of the USSR in the Middle East and in certain parts of the developing world as based on the Soviet determination to prevent the West, including the USA and Canada, from obtaining these resources. By encouraging national liberation movements which are anti-

West to gain power the USSR may be able to achieve this while promoting the spread of communism. In addition the growing worldwide presence of the Soviet naval forces heightens its capacity to threaten the trade routes by which such imports reach Northern America.

## How One Side sees the Origins and Continuation of the Cold War

**An American view**  Below is an extract from a fictional paper explaining the Cold War as might be seen by a conservative or right-wing American historian around 1950.

---

The rapid collapse in East–West relations 1945–7 was due to various Soviet actions which indicated that the Soviet Union wanted to conquer all Europe and spread communism worldwide. Major disagreement first occurred among the allies over Poland. The Russians first showed themselves hostile to the idea of a 'free' Poland after the war by killing some four thousand captured Polish officers and civilians whose graves were discovered by the Germans in the Katyn Forest in early 1943. Then the Russians delayed their liberation of the Polish capital until the Warsaw uprising in 1944 had been ruthlessly suppressed by the Germans.

After the war the Russians refused to continue to co-operate with the West. This was illustrated by the continual use of the 'veto' by the USSR in the Security Council of the United Nations to block action being taken to defend world peace. Shortly after the Potsdam meeting the Russians stopped all movement of people and of communications, for example news broadcasts between East and West Europe. This barrier or Iron Curtain between Soviet-controlled Eastern Europe and Western Europe stretched some 1800 miles from Lubeck in North Germany to Trieste.

Further evidence of the 'lack of good faith' of the Russians and their determination not to respect agreements or the peace treaties was their encouragement to the efforts of various communist parties to seize power in Turkey, Italy and Greece, and their obstruction of any efforts to unite Germany, as in the Berlin blockade (1948–9) while extracting heavy reparation payments not only from East but also from West Germany.

---

## Against Pacifism

There is a view that insists that pacifism and the reluctance to fight is a form of cowardice. Some people would prefer a 'hot war' to a 'cold' one.

---

Such good as exists in the world – including Christianity – and such few cases of civilisation . . . are due to the marvellous willingness of a few brave men to fight to the death.

Without the willingness of such brave men to go to war, it would be the peace of the Devil that had long since reigned on earth, not the peace of God.

Pacifism is a vice, not a virtue, a lie, not the truth.

The advent of nuclear weapons has greatly increased the temptation to pacifism. . . . Never has it been so easy for the apathetic to find plausible excuses to sanctify their apathy.

Peregrine Worsthorne, 'Why pacifism brings a smile to the Devil', Sunday Telegraph, 8 August 1982.

## Better Dead than Red

'Better dead than red' is a slogan which has several meanings. If it means that one should risk one's life rather than submit to communism, then it expresses a sentiment which is shared by all those who, like myself, believe that it would be right to fight and die in a conventional war against a communist invasion. Some might go further, and believe that one should die rather than submit to communist rule. Someone might hold this in the extreme form of believing that one should kill oneself rather than fall into communist hands.

Anthony Kenny, The Logic of Deterrence, 1985

## Better Red than Dead

If a nuclear holocaust is the alternative to a communist victory then it is better to submit to communism in the short term. Some Christians, followers of other faiths and agnostics have argued on moral grounds that it is wrong to take innocent lives in a nuclear war, whether as the aggressor or in retaliation. Some also justify the taking of life when acting defensively in a conventional war and argue that, if the West lost such a war, the alternative to a nuclear encounter would be the various forms of alternative defence. This would help make the country inhospitable to any communist invader.

see John Stott, Issues Facing Christians Today, 1984

Parade of weapons in Moscow to celebrate the anniversary of the Russian Revolution

There is also the view that to fall under communist rule is a fate worse than death.

Vladimir Bukovsky argued in *The Times* of 4 December 1981 that Western nuclear disarmament movements like that of the 1950s or the revival of CND in the early 1980s were naive responses to Soviet propaganda which has the following purposes:

**1.** To distract attention from Soviet expansion and gains in Central Europe after 1945.

**2.** To create in Europe anti-American sentiments which are opposed to governments taking a strong anti-Soviet line in Western Europe and the USA.

**3.** To create opposition to military spending and the siting of nuclear weapons by the West, thus slowing down Western defence policies.

---
## ACTIVITIES
---

**1.** Explain clearly the meaning or purpose of the following  **(a)** moratorium **(b)** reparations  **(c)** Iron Curtain.

**2.** **(a)** Was the Cold War inevitable? How do you think it could have been avoided?

**(b)** How might a 'cold war' lead to a 'hot' one?

**3.** Do you agree that it is better to be 'dead' than 'red'? Why does Solzhenitsyn (page 93) take the view that to be 'red' is to be 'dead' anyway? Is there any truth in the claims of Peregrine Worsthorne (pages 92–3)?

# 6.2  Western Nuclear Strategy and the Arms Race

From 1945 the West had no clear military defence strategy in the Cold War, initially because of the American monopoly of nuclear power. Even after the Russians acquired nuclear weapons much earlier than expected, the United States retained immense superiority.

**The massive response strategy**  The Russians and the Warsaw Pact allies were in a stronger position to fight a conventional war than the USA and Nato, having more troops and tanks. Under Foster Dulles, American Secretary of State, the United States developed the plan from the mid to the late 1950s of meeting any local attack by the USSR through instant and massive retaliation by American nuclear bombers against Soviet territory. At first both sides concentrated on the production of long-range heavy bombers. Eventually they came to rely on missiles, which had greater speed and so were more difficult to destroy.

**The end of American nuclear invulnerability**  In 1957 the Americans were alarmed by the Russian launching of Sputnik I, which showed that the USSR would soon be able to launch nuclear missiles against the USA. As the USSR seemed to be ahead in missiles (the 'missile gap' so called by President Kennedy in 1960 which was later found not to exist (see page 100)) this meant the USSR could launch a successful 'first-strike' attack, which would destroy the USA with one blow. (See diagram below.)

**The 'second strike' strategy (MAD)**  From the early 1960s the Americans developed the capacity to retaliate after suffering a nuclear attack, as its nuclear weapons were now put underground or undersea, for example in Polaris submarines. As the two sides now had the ability to launch a second strike, they both came to rely on deterring one another by the threat of retaliation. This was also known as the 'balance of terror' or MAD, which stood for 'mutually assured destruction'.

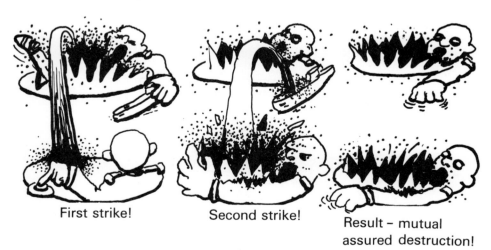

First strike!    Second strike!    Result – mutual assured destruction!

**The development of MIRVS** From 1966 to 1970 the USA began to fit ballistic missiles with a multiple independently targetable re-entry vehicle (MIRV) capable of carrying several warheads, each of which could be guided to a different target. This would increase their chances of getting through Soviet defences. The USSR developed the same capacity during the period 1968–75.

**The 'flexible response' strategy (counterforce)** In 1967 Nato more or less abandoned the 'massive retaliation' strategy in favour of one of reacting to a Soviet nuclear attack with a range of possible options ranging from the use of small to large-scale weapons aimed mainly at military targets. It also meant that, if the Soviets launched a conventional war, the West would respond by a gradual escalation of the conflict to whatever level was considered necessary to show the Warsaw Pact that Nato was determined to resist.

| Events | Date | |
|---|---|---|
| | US | USSR |
| Atomic Bomb | 1945 | 1949 |
| Intercontinental Bomber | 1948 | 1955 |
| Western Alliance (Nato) | 1949 (April) | |
| Eastern Alliance (Warsaw Pact) | | 1955 |
| Creation of West Germany | 1949 (May) | |
| Creation of East Germany | | 1949 (Oct) |
| Hydrogen Bomb | 1952 | 1953 |
| Intercontinental Ballistic Missile (ICBM). | 1958 | 1957 |
| Space Satellite | 1958 | 1957 |
| Submarine-Launched Ballistic Missile (SLBM) | 1960 | 1968 |
| First man in Space | 1962 | 1961 |
| Multiple Warhead (on missiles) or Multiple re-entry vehicle (MRV) | 1966 | 1968 |
| Anti-Ballistic Missile | 1968 | 1972 |
| Multiple Independently Targetable Re-entry Vehicle (or warhead) (MIRV) | 1970 | 1975 |
| Long-range Cruise Missile (ALCM) | 1982 | ? |
| Neutron Bomb | 1983 | ? |
| Strategic Defence Initiative (Star Wars) | 1985 | ? |

**Weakness of the Salt I talks**   The Strategic Arms Limitation Talks (Salt) between the USA and the USSR from 1972 aimed to set upper limits to the number of missiles, but little attention was paid to the number of warheads on each missile. This accounts for the fast growth in multiple warhead missiles held by both superpowers during the 1970s.

Salt I did not limit cruise missiles, which explains their rapid development in the United States in the 1970s. Their accuracy and non-detectability by radar meant that they could be used for a 'first strike'.

By the late 1970s many Western military experts came to believe that the Warsaw Pact was not only superior to the West in many aspects of potential conventional warfare but also in many areas of nuclear weapons. This was a factor which led the US President in 1980 to increase American arms spending and Nato's decision to strengthen its ability to fight a war, whether nuclear or non-nuclear.

## Causes of the East–West Arms Race

1.   Traditional explanations for past 'arms races' focus on factors *external* to any particular country, such as various international tensions, or on unresolved problems or rivalries involving two or more countries. Mutual fear and suspicion play a part in the building up of arms, each side inter-preting its own actions as defensive and the actions of the other as aggressive. (See cartoon below.)

# Armaments don't give security

*Quaker Peace and Service*

One solution is for one side to try to lower tension by a disarmament measure which will break the arms spiral. However during the period of *détente* or calm which followed the Cuban Crisis (1962) the arms race continued. Arms control measures tended to be ineffective, being largely confined to lines of development which neither side thought productive, for example the Anti-Ballistic Missile Agreement.

**2.** As a result some observers concluded that the source of the Cold War arms race was not so much the result of international tensions, or external factors, as *domestic or internal* factors, such as the influence of special groups including the military. President Eisenhower had already drawn people's attention to this development in January 1961 when he warned Americans to guard against the unwarranted influence in government of the 'military–industrial complex'. (See the explanation provided by Frank Barnaby below.)

---

It seems to me that the mess we are in because of the uncontrolled nuclear arms race can be explained simply by the enormous political lobbying power of those groups in the USA and the USSR which continuously press for the use of all possibly technologies for military purposes.

The four main groups involved are the military (any group which disposes of $550,000 million a year is bound to have immense political power); the defence industry (which grosses about $130,000 million a year – the second biggest world business after oil); the academics (about 40% of the world's scientists are funded from military budgets); and the bureaucrats (about 27 million civilians work for defence establishments).

Political leaders know that if they resist the demands of these groups they will be thrown out of office or not re-elected. Since, by their very nature, they want more than anything to remain in power, they give in.

Frank Barnaby, 'UNA's great responsibility', New World — Disarmament and SSD2.

---

In turn the influence of these special groups partly explains the continuous attempt to modernise and update weapon systems and the growth of the arms trade itself.

## ———— ACTIVITIES ————

1. Find examples from past history where arms races have been contributory factors causing wars. Note in particular the Anglo–German naval arms race which preceded the First World War.

2. Study the two cartoons relating to the arms race and also the chart describing developments in weapons since 1945 on page 96. In pairs discuss how they can

be used to support both  (a) mutual fear and suspicion and  (b) the 'military–industrial complex' as contributory causes of the present nuclear arms race.

3.  Explain how Frank Barnaby describes the four main groups comprising the 'military–industrial complex'. Provide more details about these actual groups.

4.  Suggest what possible options might be available to the NATO Commander-in-Chief if Western Europe was attacked by Soviet conventional forces. Refer to Alternative Defence, pages 86–7, when considering your answer.

5.  Comment in a short one-page essay, giving historical examples, on the following statement:

> Certainly armaments races can exacerbate international tensions, but they are as much the consequences of those tensions as the cause.

*Michael Howard*

---

# The Nuclear Numbers Game

Understanding the statistics behind the bombs

RADICAL STATISTICS NUCLEAR DISARMAMENT GROUP

*Radical Statistics Nuclear Disarmament Group, 1982*

**World Nuclear Weapons**

| | Strategic | Intermediate | Tactical | **Total:** |
|---|---|---|---|---|
| **US** | 10,000 | 1,300 | 17,700 | **29,000** |
| **USSR** | 7,400 | 3,500 | 6,500 | **17,400** |
| **UK** | 192 | 96 | 158 | **446** |
| **France** | 80 | 18 | 165 | **263** |
| **China** | 4 | 200 | 100 | **304** |
| **Totals** | 17,676 | 5,114 | 24,623 | **47,413** |

**Strategic** – capable of intercontinental distances and/or intended for use against the enemy's homeland.
**Intermediate** – range or combat radius of 1,500 miles or more.
**Tactical** – all other shorter range or battlefield systems, including land mines and artillery shells.
**Weapons** – warheads and bombs.

*Australian Catholic Review, 1984*

# New Technology

The continuous efforts of government scientists and manufacturers to improve weapons systems and to devise effective defences against other people's new weapons has been a major feature of the superpower arms race. A new weapons system may take more than five years from start to finish. Naturally manufacturers are keen on new developments to gain contracts and more business, while politicians want to preserve jobs for their voters, and each branch of the armed forces wants the most up-to-date equipment.

To justify producing weapons which will not be ready for many years, military leaders, politicians or manufacturers may take a very pessimistic view of the future and exaggerate the 'threat' to their country. An example was the famous so-called 'missile gap' which worried Americans in the late 1950s. This was based on reports from the US air force on photographs brought back from high-flying spy planes that the USSR would have 100 intercontinental ballistic missiles (ICBMs) by 1960 and the USA only 30. Later evidence showed that these estimates were wrong and that in 1961 the Russians had only four ICBMs.

Statistics may be manipulated to prove that one side has more or better weapons than the other in order to justify increased arms spending, as President Reagan did to get approval for the MX missile project.

# The Arms Trade

As the two superpowers, supported by their allies, are in competition for power and influence, they believe that it is in their own interests to supply arms to friendly countries. Their reasons include the following:

1.    The arms trade helps a country's exports and balance of payments, while the sale of obsolete weapons assists finance research and development on new weapons.

2.    The arms trade enables the gaining of allies which will reduce the influence of a rival power. For example the USA supplies arms to anti-communist governments such as South Korea, El Salvador, Pakistan and Israel. The USSR supplies arms to movements trying to overthrow Western-style capitalist governments, and to anti-American countries such as Cuba or Libya.

3.    The arms trade helps each side in the Cold War obtain military facilities such as airports, military bases and harbours.

Sometimes it is military dictatorships which buy the arms which increases their capacity to wage war or to control civil unrest or revolts against unjust rule.

**Arms exporters, 1979–81**

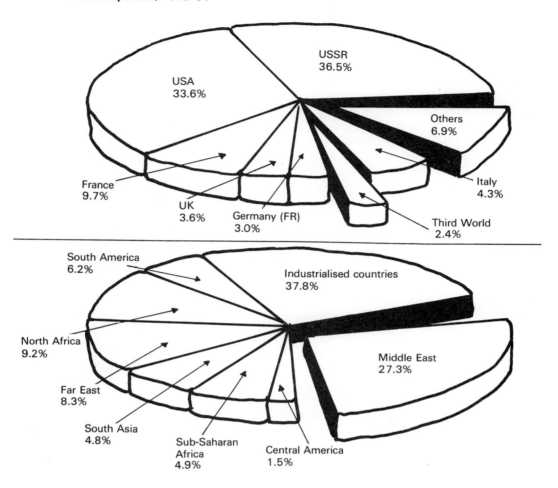

**Main arms importing regions, 1979–81**

*Stockholm International Peace Research Institute Yearbook 1982*

## ACTIVITIES

1.  Using the diagrams above, answer the following:

    (a) which country was the third largest arms exporter?

    (b) which area was the largest arms importing region? Give reasons why this should be so.

2.  Give examples since 1960 of military dictatorships or oppressive governments which have used arms imports from the USA partly to maintain their rule and put down revolts. Why do you think they were able to obtain these weapons from the USA?

# 6.3   Arms and Disarmament – The Various Positions

## The Rearmers or Retentionists

This group completely distrusts the USSR and believes that Russian disarmament proposals are intended to divide the West or are aimed at the one area where the West might have superior strength. The West must maintain its present defence systems, or continually increase and modernise its arms to maintain equality with the USSR or to secure an edge or 'lead' over the Eastern bloc. This group tends to advocate the balance of power and deterrence theories, or MAD. (See page 95.)

## Multilateralists

In Britain, the Conservatives, the Labour Party (until 1982) and the SDP–Liberal Alliance all support this approach. Two broad divisions are:

**1.**   Those who support general disarmament negotiations

The hope is that a single treaty will be reached by which governments agree on the total reduction of arms and arms production capacity of individual states to the level needed for internal security, and to support UN peace forces. Sensitive borders might be patrolled by means of an internationally controlled peacekeeping force.

**2.**   Those who favour gradual disarmament

Gradual disarmament would take place through various agreements ('small steps') taken regarding arms in various areas. Limited multilateral agreements have been reached on the following:

- making Antarctica a nuclear-free zone (1959)
- a partial test ban (1963)
- the prohibition of nuclear weapons in Latin America (1967)
- the prohibition of nuclear weapons in outer space (1967)
- nuclear non-proliferation (1968)
- no nuclear tests on the sea bed (1971)
- non-use of bacteriological weapons (1972)
- prohibition of 'environmental modification' (1977) bans the use of methods to change the weather or other aspects of the environment for hostile purposes

The Thatcher government since 1979 has generally favoured option 2.

The illustration from the news-sheet *The Balanced View* issued by the Arms Control and Disarmament Research Unit, London, illustrates the government view that real disarmament can only take place when both sides decide to disarm simultaneously.

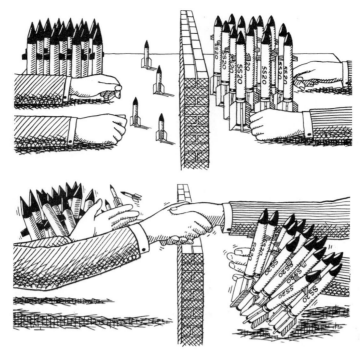

The Balanced View, *HMSO, 1984*

The extract below is from a government pamphlet showing its own multi-lateralist position and its view of the unilateralist position.

## What the Unilateralists Say

**2** Nuclear weapons are so destructive that conquest would be preferable to annihilation: 'better red than dead'. Britain should renounce nuclear weapons in order to give a moral lead to others.

### Nuclear War

**9** We are on the brink of a nuclear holocaust. There are now so many nuclear weapons in the world that nuclear war is inevitable. Nuclear weapons represent the most immediate threat to humanity.

**10** Renouncing our nuclear weapons will reduce the risk of war. A nuclear-free Britain would be safe from attack.

## What the Multilateralists Say

If we maintain adequate defences and negotiate for arms reductions, we can preserve peace *and* freedom. Unilateral action by the UK would not reduce the nuclear weapons held by the USSR, US, France or China. Nor is there any moral gain in renouncing nuclear weapons, yet sheltering under the nuclear protection of the US.

All weapons of war threaten humanity. The decisive factor is not the size of the arsenals but the behaviour of governments. Deterrence continues to make nuclear war most unlikely. But 150 conflicts with conventional weapons have taken over 10 million lives since 1945.

Unilateral disarmament invites aggression and so increases the risk of war. Without nuclear weapons Britain would face a greater threat of conventional attack, as well as nuclear blackmail.

*Foreign and Commonwealth Office, 1982*

# PEACE AND THE ROUTE TO DISARMAMENT

## BALANCED (MULTILATERAL) DISARMAMENT

The objective of the Conservative Government is to maintain Peace with Freedom. At the same time it is anxious to secure major measures of actual arms *reductions*, nuclear and conventional, by both sides.

## ONE-SIDED DISARMAMENT (UNILATERALISM)

### – The road to disaster

It was the one-sided disarmament by Britain in the 1930s, (encouraged by the 'peace' movements) that persuaded Hitler that he could attack the democracies with impunity and so led us into World War II – a holocaust in which 50 million people were killed by conventional weapons.

If Britain unilaterally abandoned its nuclear weapons – or denied the United States the use of bases, which have contributed to the maintenance of our peace and security for 30 years – we could be repeating the same mistake in a nuclear age, inviting catastrophe.

Control of the United Kingdom would be essential for Soviet mastery of Europe. In the face of the continuing Soviet arms build-up, unilateral action would *increase* the possibility of a Soviet attack, either with nuclear weapons or with their superiod strength of conventional weaponry.

## THE RIGHT HONOURABLE MARGARET THATCHER MP
*Prime Minister*

'Despite regular reminders of the ruthless actions of the Kremlin, there are still those who seem to believe that disarmament by ourselves alone would so impress the Russians that they would obligingly follow suit!

'I understand the anxieties of parents with children growing up in the nuclear age. But the fundamental question for all of us is whether unilateral disarmament would make war less likely. I have to tell you that it would not. It would make war more likely ...'
(Brighton, October 1982)

'I believe that the duty of government is both to ensure the survival of the State and to bear witness to the moral basis which is necessary for a free society.' (**The Bishop of London**, 3rd November 1982)

'It's got to be a mutually agreed and verifiable disarmament. I think it would be disaster for one country to disarm and put themselves at the mercy of the other.'
(**Dr. Billy Graham**, 7th May 1982)

'Let no one expect a unilateral disarmament from us. We are not a naive people.' (**Mr. Andropov**, Financial Times, 23rd November 1982)

### THE CONCEPT OF DETERRENCE

Those who advocate one-sided disarmament claim the presence of nuclear weapons on British soil makes us a target. As the Soviets' unprovoked aggression against Afghanistan makes clear, we are all potential targets of Soviet attack. It should never be forgotten that it was specifically because Japan did *not* have nuclear weapons that the people of Hiroshima and Nagasaki became the victims of nuclear attack.

Nuclear weapons cannot be disinvented. Our task must be to ensure a system for living in peace and freedom in which nuclear weapons are never used, either to destroy or to blackmail.

'Deterrence' is a simple message: 'Do not attack me, because if you do, I can and will fight back and hurt you enough to make you wish you had never started the fight!'

A weak deterrent (for instance, one which did not remain modern and technologically advanced) would cease to be effective. Hence the need for NATO to update its systems with Cruise and for Britain to replace its Polaris submarines with Trident. Until unbalanced 'multilateral' disarmament is achieved, there can be no safer path to peace.

*Extract from pamphlet by Campaign for Defence and Multilateral Disarmament*

**Cummings**

Sunday Express, *12 December 1982*

The Soviet Union is a country obsessed with its own security, but unable to acknowledge the potential threat that its massive forces pose to others. We shall carry on working to build the trust needed to make progress. But it is essential that the Western nations continue to provide a sufficient counterweight to Soviet strength. . . . The ideology on which the Soviet Union is based has not changed fundamentally. Nor has its desire to extend its strength and influence world-wide. . . . Nato aims to demonstrate to any aggressor beyond all doubt that the risks of using or threatening force against any of the Nato countries are simply too great. . . . Nuclear weapons will remain fundamental to Nato strategy for the foreseeable future. The best conventional forces in the world would be useless against an opponent who could threaten a nuclear strike without fear of retaliation.

*Ministry of Defence booklet, 1986*

**Deterrent** Anything which uses the motive of fear to turn someone from a course of action. Deterrence is the main argument in defence, at different levels, of corporal punishment, capital punishment and nuclear power. It would be idle to pretend that deterrents never deter: but they tend to create new problems. There is evidence, for example, that capital punishment, while deterring some, leads others to violence, either out of self-directed death-instinct, or by force of example of violence.

Nuclear deterrence has kept the peace for 40 years, and a non-nuclear world would be much more dangerous. The temptation for the superpowers to use some of the many nasty conventional chemical or biological weapons at their disposal would be increased, which would leave Western Europe very vulnerable indeed to Soviet attack. And any Colonel Gadaffi who managed to obtain a nuclear weapon could hold the rest of us to ransom.

*Editorial*, Sunday Times, *19 January 1986*

## The Bilateralists

This group believes that since 95 per cent of the world's nuclear weapons are in the hands of the two superpowers, both the USA and the USSR should take the lead by signing a bilateral agreement not to test, produce or deploy nuclear weapons. This would be the first step in lessening the nuclear threat, and could be followed by an international conference to agree on multilateral disarmament. This approach was recommended by the Chinese Foreign Minister, Wu Xueqian, in his speech to the UN General Assembly, September 1983, and the American peace movements during a demonstration in New York, 12 June 1983 when nearly a million people supported a nuclear freeze.

Examples of this approach have included the 1963 'hot line' between the White House and the Kremlin; the 1971 agreement for both the USA and USSR to notify each other in case of nuclear accidents; 1972 Salt II agreed to limit the number of ABMs deployed) and to place a five-year freeze on the total number of ballistic-missile launchers.

Trust cannot be acquired by means of force. Nor can it be obtained by declarations alone. Trust must be won with concrete acts and facts.

*Pope John Paul II, 1 January 1980*

## The Unilateralists

Some groups, such as the Campaign for Nuclear Disarmament in Britain, advocate that each country should disarm independently. Unilateral disarmament is not seen as the ultimate goal, but as a means to bring about multilateral disarmament. (For CND's arguments, see Chapter 11.)

# British Opinion on the Arms Race and East–West Relations (MORI poll)

According to the Market and Opinion Research International (MORI) poll carried out for the BBC and reported in *The Times* (25 November 1981) 69 per cent of the population oppose unilateralism and only 23 per cent support it. Unilateral disarmament was opposed by 86 per cent of the Conservatives, 69 per cent of the SDP–Liberal Alliance, and 56 per cent of Labour supporters. An independent British nuclear deterrent was favoured by 52 per cent of the respondents. Respondents aged between 15 and 24 were the most likely to support unilateralism (29 per cent). Less than half of those interviewed (40 per cent) believed the United States genuinely wanted world peace, and only 6 per cent felt the same way about the USSR. Only 22 per cent felt the Americans could be trusted to keep their word on nuclear disarmament, and only 5 per cent thought the Russians could.

## ═══ ACTIVITIES ═══

1. Discover the four main arguments from the extracts on the preceding pages which defend or support the belief that the West should retain nuclear weapons.

2. What are the strengths and weaknesses of the 'deterrence' theory?

3. Hold a discussion to find to what extent members of your group or class would agree or disagree with the findings of the MORI poll above.

4.       If you want peace, prepare for war.

   Write a short essay or discuss in a group how true or false this statement is. Would you agree that multilateralists would generally support this view, and that unilateralists would not?

5. Devise two posters in support of the following: **(a)** a campaign to make a year's military training for young people compulsory by law; **(b)** a campaign to encourage young people voluntarily to do a year's community or social service work in Britain and overseas. Find out why France has compulsory military service and Britain does not.

# 7 CONFLICT SOLVING – INDIVIDUALS AND SMALL GROUPS

## 7.1 Peace Skills

People who are self-confident, cheerful and extrovert by nature tend to find it easier to make friends than others. Lonely people are inclined to be withdrawn and nervous, have difficulty in making friends or in holding lengthy conversations.

Relationship skills include self-confidence and assertiveness, the ability to communicate with others and to empathise, that is to see other people and societies from their perspective and one's own society from the viewpoint of others. Also important are open-mindedness, caring and appreciation of, and interest in, others. These skills are also those necessary for coping with conflict situations in which we are personally involved, or for helping others as intermediaries resolve theirs. In particular avoiding conflict or handling it constructively entails skills relating to communication, assertiveness and co-operation.

---

No peace in the world without peace in the nation;
No peace in the nation without peace in the town;
No peace in the town without peace in the home;
No peace in the home without peace in the heart.

*Tao Te Ching*

---

A story told to children of earlier generations spoke of a small boy who was given a difficult jigsaw puzzle picturing a map of the world. Having been unsuccessful in assembling the map of the world he turned to the picture on the back which proved much easier, being of a man. When it was finished he turned the whole picture over and there was the map of the world. The moral was – 'get the man right, and you will have the world right'.

---

# Three Definitions of Peace

A state of peace can mean many things. A good dictionary would help you see some of the concepts and ideas linked to this word, such as peace of mind, happiness or bliss, which do not all mean the same thing. Three broad approaches to peace are called negative peace, positive peace and peace as harmony or balance.

**Negative peace**   This is the absence of war or direct, physical violence. It reflects the conventional view of peace which conforms with the meaning of the Latin word *pax*, an agreement not to fight.

The chief method of ensuring negative peace does not differ from the normal method of stopping a street brawl – those involved are physically separated. The United Nations has performed this role in a number of peacekeeping operations in areas of conflict such as the Middle East. Examples are given in Chapter 10 and the drawbacks of this approach to peace are outlined.

**Positive peace**   Just as pills may help make a patient feel better rather than curing him, so the ability to stop a conflict does not necessarily mean that the conflict is solved.

Positive peace focuses on removing the causes rather than the symptoms of a sickness like war, violence and crime. This is the approach adopted by UN organisations such as the ILO (International Labour Organisation), WHO (World Health Organisation) and UNESCO. The belief is that real peace is only possible when the underlying injustices (structural violence) which make for unpeaceful relations between states, classes and all peoples are removed.

*Yin–Yang symbol*

**Peace as harmony or balance**   The Chinese word ping, meaning peace, conveys no idea of stopping conflict, but implies a harmony of opposites brought about by adjustment. This is conveyed by the Taoist symbol of Yin–Yang (female–male). Yin represents all that is gentle, tender, loving, co-operative, sensitive, caring, intuitive, dark, feminine, imaginative, mystical and lunar. In contrast Yang represents all that is strong, efficient, objective, rational, bright, solar, competitive, male and practical. When the two are in proper balance, as in mature individuals and communities, harmony reigns.

# Assertiveness and Affirmation

Assertive people do not allow themselves to be pushed around or 'put down' by others. In other words they do not accept unfair criticism or treatment. Sometimes in dealing with anti-social behaviour, bullying or racist behaviour for example, the only answer is effective confrontation or 'head-on' conflict to settle the matter once and for all, to avoid future repetition. Assertive skills include the ability to be forthright, without being aggressive, to appear relaxed, and to talk clearly but not too loudly to someone else while keeping eye contact.

If a person has a poor or negative self-image and lacks confidence, it is difficult for that person to feel positive towards others, or to see their point of view. If an individual affirms or says something good or encouraging about another, boosting his or her morale, this helps in breaking down prejudices and negative images and in creating an atmosphere of goodwill and trust between groups in conflict.

Affirmation can be demonstrated in various ways of which the following are examples:

1. Finding ways of agreeing with/praising/thanking others rather than disagreeing with or condemning them.

2. Using non-verbal gestures effectively to befriend others or diffuse a conflict situation, such as smiles, friendly tone or voice, welcoming manner, touching.

3. Using the right words and manner – kind and sympathetic, not critical, hostile or superior.

# Clear Thinking and the Open Mind

Clear thinking helps us to be creative and open-minded, to cope better with problems and to find solutions to the difficulties encountered in life.

Tendencies of the open and creative mind include:

1. **Adopting a many-sided rather than a black and white approach**   Problems and issues do not necessarily have clear answers, that is for or against, good or bad, wrong or right associated with polarised thinking. Instead a person might be neutral or impartial, indifferent or have a view but is not prone to dogmatism. Instead, the person is able to see right and wrong on both sides, and also believes that there are many ways of looking at the matter, even though not all viewpoints are equally valid.

2. **Being flexible and broadminded**   This involves being receptive to new ideas and knowledge of the facts supporting different viewpoints. Thus you are not prejudiced or stereotyped, but change your views in the light of new evidence.

**3.  Not letting emotions influence thinking unduly**  Edward de Bono in his book *De Bono's Thinking Course* argues in favour of working on hunches, gut feelings and emotions if used at the end of thinking on a problem, but not as a substitute for it.

**4.  Relating things and ideas which seem unconnected**  You will notice that some humour, advertising and much of modern art illustrate aspects of lateral thinking, the linking together of things which appear to be unrelated.

---

It is well to open one's mind but only as a preliminary to closing it

*Irving Babbitt*

If you keep your mind sufficiently open people will throw a lot of rubbish into it

*William A Orton*

---

## Techniques for a Constructive Argument

Sometimes when emotions and tempers are high, members of a group may cease listening to one another, and respond in an angry manner. The result is a 'dialogue of the deaf' and neither side appreciates what it is like to be 'in the shoes of their opponent'. Alternatively, a guest in your parents' house might say something with which you disagree, and it would be unwise or tactless to argue with this person. Some of the methods which could be used to encourage an orderly, friendly discussion rather than a bitter argument can be listed as guidelines for 'fighting fair'.

### Do's

**1.  Identify and discuss the relevant issue**  It may emerge that there is really nothing to disagree about. So as to avoid misunderstandings and to allow immediate correction of inaccuracies in communication, the listener can repeat what has just been said in summary form. He then makes his own comment in reply. The need for a listener to summarise or state more precisely what has just been said is useful if the previous speaker was rather confused or long-winded in his comment. The listener can then ask: 'Is that it?' Alternatively the listener may ask for clarification: 'Can you repeat that'? or ask a fact-finding or probing question: 'Where or how did you find this out?'

**2.  Allow a breathing space to 'cool down'**  Once a person has calmed down, he might see the situation in a different light, or choose to forget it. Possibly an interval of silence can be allowed between responses in a heated debate so that participants can reflect on the previous contribution and control their own emotions before replying.

**3.  Attack the issue, not the person**  Try to work with each other to find the truth instead of against each other. When you reject someone's opinion, try to show that you are not rejecting that person: 'I appreciate your views, but I believe that . . .' Sometimes a non-committal reply can be made: 'Oh yes, why do you think that?' or 'Why do such things happen?'

**4.   Argue at the right moment**   A sensitive topic should not be brought up at an inappropriate time, for example in front of guests, when there is insufficient time to discuss it, or when both are tired.

**5.   Argue with the right person and over the right problem**   (See number 7 under Don'ts.)

**6.   Listen**   Often people are so busy thinking of their reply that they do not really hear or understand what has been said. Try to appreciate the experiences that have brought the speaker to his or her present viewpoint.

**7.   Be willing to compromise**   Chances are that neither person is 100 per cent right or wrong. Look for the element of truth in your opponent's position.

**8.   Learn from experience and criticisms**   Sift through insults, allowing for misunderstandings, and see if they have any justification. If they do, try to make any needed changes in yourself.

**9.   Make peace**   If you cannot reach an agreement, disagree amicably. Apologise for anything unfair or mean you may have said.

**Don'ts**

**1.   Avoid personal verbal abuse**   (insults and 'name calling').

**2.   Don't act superior to your opponent**   If he or she appears to be losing the argument, it is unnecessary to use lots of facts and figures to prove your point when one fact or piece of information will do.

**3.   Don't sidetrack**   In other words, do not 'muckrake' by bringing up the past or reminding your opponent of mistakes which have no real bearing on the current disagreement.

**4.   Avoid 'put down' remarks**   Certain sarcastic, unkind or unfeeling remarks may make another feel small, embarrassed or regret having spoken.

**5.   Avoid 'stamp collecting'**   This is the listing of little incidents which caused annoyance in the past and, instead of discussing them at the time, waiting until a big argument or row occurs before mentioning them. This habit breeds distrust and lack of confidence. One remedy is to express displeasure about incidents at the time they occur.

**6.   Avoid generalisations**   such as 'Parents always . . .' or 'Teachers never . . .'

**7.   Avoid 'scape-goating'**   There is no point in getting angry with an innocent party (for example the boss, wife, sister or brother, the dog) when you are afraid or unable to argue with the culprit or person responsible for your anger.

# ACTIVITIES

1. We can start an exploration of what 'peace' means by looking at peace and violence in our lives. A useful device is a time line which covers our past life up to the present. Draw such a line and mark off along it instances or periods which were violent or peaceful.

2. Write down something complimentary or pleasant about **(a)** each member of your class **(b)** the following nationalities or cultures: English, French, Welsh, Jamaican, Japanese, Polish, Brazilian, Rastafarian, Pakistani.

3. Think of ways of making a friend who is sad happy or laugh. Find a joke that will make him or her smile.

4. Hold a group thinking session and make a list of negative ('put-down') and positive words. Then hold two-person interviews, where the interviewer asks questions and is expected to affirm the other as much as possible.

5. Make a list of controversial statements likely to provoke an argument. Suggest the kind of responses likely to lead to a constructive discussion, and the kind which might lead to a bitter row or a 'dirty fight'. An example might be a member of your family saying to a guest in your house at dinner: 'I think all people who commit terrorist attacks should be hanged, don't you?'

6. Find some passages from the Bible which relate to the theme of 'fighting fair'. (Examples: Matthew 5:21,25 Ephesians 4:25,27.)

7. Explain under what sort of conditions you or another person might use one of the following ways for dealing with a problem or conflict situation:

   **(a)** avoid the person

   **(b)** change the subject

   **(c)** try to understand the other person's view

   **(d)** turn the conflict into a joke

   **(e)** give in and apologise

   **(f)** try to compromise

   **(g)** pretend to agree

   **(h)** get outside help

   **(i)** threaten the other person

   **(j)** fight

   **(k)** complain until you get your way

8. Small groups could devise situations of two-party conflict (two friends having a quarrel) or of two people plus a mediator, which they could prepare in advance. Then the confrontation could be acted in the middle of a circle with the rest of the group watching. At the end of each role play (or possibly at the end of the session) the group gives the views on **(a)** how the conflict was handled and ended **(b)** whether any alternatives would have been preferable and why. (Refer to Chapter 10, page 172.)

9. Lateral thinking and clear thinking:

(a) Discover five uses for a paper clip other than clipping paper.

(b) How many squares are there if one large square is divided into 16 smaller squares of equal size?

(c) Read the sentence below once. Then count the number of Fs. Count them once only. Discuss in pairs why different people might give different answers.

> FINISHED FILES ARE THE RE-
> SULT OF YEARS OF SCIENTIF-
> IC STUDY COMBINED WITH THE
> EXPERIENCE OF MANY YEARS

10. If two members of your class at a school, normally great friends, had a bitter dispute and came close to a fist fight, what arguments or techniques might you use to try to persuade them to settle their dispute peacefully?

## 7.2 Working for Peace

### What You Can Do to Help

Either individually, or with your family, friends or as part of an organisation, you might be able to play a small part in making the world a better and safer place. Through reading material provided by various peace or other organisations which interest you, through discussion with others and through research in your local library, you should obtain suitable ideas. In addition you will gain ideas from this chapter and the rest of the book, apart from the few modest suggestions outlined below.

1. Increase your knowledge of local, national and world affairs.

2. Take part in voluntary charitable and social service activities.

3. Help fund-raising for good causes, for example sponsored walks.

4. Live simply.

5. Help publicise important issues, for example distribute leaflets, hold an exhibition, start a letter-writing campaign or undertake street petitioning.

6. Join a local/national group concerned about some aspect of world issues and problems, for example peace, the environment, the Third World.

**Getting started** We can always find plenty of excuses for not doing something. No doubt you could make a lengthy list of negative statements illustrating apathy and narrow-mindedness in this field. Examples are the following:

● I haven't time to bother about other things or such people. I am busy looking after my family and myself.

- There is nothing I can do as an individual to make the world any different.
- American and Soviet leaders would not be stupid enough to start a nuclear war.
- It does not matter what happens elsewhere in the world. Let's worry only about what goes on in our own country or community.

The remaining extracts in this sub-section deal with this problem of 'getting started' and reasons why your individual participation could make a difference.

---

The main character in a fictional war story explains his position to a psychiatrist: 'From now on I'm thinking only of me'.
Major Danby replied indulgently with a superior smile: 'But, Yossarian, suppose everyone felt that way'.
'Then', said Yossarian, 'I'd certainly be a damned fool to feel any other way, wouldn't I?'

*Joseph Heller,* Catch 22, *1964*

---

**The Hundred Monkey Phenomenon**   Using monkeys as an example in a story, Ken Keyes in *The Hundredth Monkey* (1981) argues that when only a limited number of people know of something, then nothing happens. However a point is reached as in the old saying 'the last straw which broke the camel's back' when, if only one more person also becomes aware of this thing, then this awareness is picked up by almost everyone!

**The Power of the Weak**   'When they are united, the weak become powerful.' Just as the tiny Lilliputians in Swift's *Gulliver's Travels* were able to bind Gulliver with their gossamer-threads so, it is argued, the co-operation of the world's smaller states offers a way of bringing influence to bear on the great powers in questions of disarmament and arms control.

At the individual level the above point is relevant. Gavin Scott in his book *How to get rid of the Bomb* (1982) argues that it is only a few hundred people who tell us that we need nuclear weapons, and preparing bunkers for themselves for when the holocaust comes. However, there are millions who are paying for these weapons and, though there is little each of us as individuals can do, if we work together we may succeed in getting rid of nuclear weapons altogether.

---

'The only thing necessary for the triumph of evil is for good men to do nothing.'

*Edmund Burke*

---

*World Disarmament Campaign*

No amount of politics will change this fact, say the Indian philosophers. The world as you normally see it will never be at peace because as you normally see it the world is nothing but diversity and change.

There can be no real peace with ego, because by its nature ego is constantly opposing itself to everything else.

You will only find real peace when you realize there's a greater unity.

To do that you must be prepared to surrender ego. How?

There's an old technique called *sacrifice*.

sacrifice        peace

Sacrifice comes in 2 parts:
    letting go (detachment)
    & giving ('love' is you like)

People try to become part of something bigger than themselves by sacrificing to it. They may sacrifice their energies to their tribe or a cause and discover they are brave and strong.

But they are still not quite safe because their group may be beaten — (egoism has been stretched to encompass the tribe but it hasn't been completely snapped.)

It's only when you sacrifice yourSELF to something VAST that can't be beaten — God or the All — that ego loses its grip on you, you lose your separation and *there is peace*. That's the theory.

Some version of these ideas is present in most religions but they were most popularized by a Nepalese princeling (called the Buddha) and a young Palestinian carpenter (called Jesus) who are said to have found world religions 'of peace'.

So we can contrive another formula to add to the first (which went: groupism (division) + power = war)

UNIVERSALITY (unity) + SACRIFICE = PEACE

*Ian Kellas*, Peace for Beginners, *1984*

# Peace Movements

Most peace movements have originated in Europe and North America since 1918. Some are confined mainly to certain countries or regions. For example the World Council for Peace exists mainly in the Eastern bloc, with branches elsewhere. Some are primarily religious groups such as the Inter-ecclesiastical Council for Peace, created in 1966 by the Catholic and Protestant churches.

## Three main categories

**1.  Against war in general.** The major organisations in Britain in this field are the Peace Pledge Union, the Quakers (a peace church called also the Religious Society of Friends), Fellowship of Reconciliation, Pax Christi (branch of the Catholic church). Many pacifists or conscientious objectors belong to them.

**2.  Against particular wars.** The Committee of 100 emerged in 1960 to prevent a nuclear war between the USA and the USSR, while a mass movement started in the 1960s in the United States against the Vietnam War. This was symbolised by the refusal of many young Americans to be drafted into the armed forces and the first widely-known draft card burning in 1965.

The Peace People in Northern Ireland not only want to end the fighting and urban terrorism but have broader aims to reform totally the institutions of that area so as to end structural violence against the Catholic minority.

**3.  Against categories or aspects of war.** Examples are two pressure groups, (a) the Campaign for Nuclear Disarmament (CND) (b) Campaign Against the Arms Trade (CAAT).

**Broader aims to promote positive peace**  Some members of peace groups support the ecology movement, humanitarian causes or advocates of an alternative society as a means of building a peaceful society.

Examples are Greenpeace, Oxfam and the National Council for Civil Liberties. Certain people, whether pacifists or believers in non-violent means to achieve their aims, such as Gandhi, were not directly connected with a peace movement, in so far as such a movement was involved in the struggle to achieve negative peace as described above in the three main categories. However, they were certainly involved in the struggle to create a peaceful and just society, and to end forms of oppression or structural violence.

*War Resisters' International*

## Non-Violence in Action

This sub-section provides some examples of passive resistance and civil disobedience campaigns, demonstrations and non-violent activities which have been undertaken in various parts of the world.

---

### THE SNAKE WHO DID NOT HISS

According to one Indian legend, a snake was converted by a holy man, and promised never to bite another human being. The villagers took advantage of this and attacked it with sticks and stones. The angry snake complained to the guru who replied: 'but I never told you not to hiss'.

---

### CHILDREN OF THE WORLD UNITED

Children in Italy have petitioned their country's President for stronger legislation against the production of war toys. Owners of toy gun factories should be made to convert to the production of non-violent, socially useful goods, the President was told by petitioners who brought the signatures of 3000 of their fellow classmates.

Times Educational Supplement, *2 July 1982*

---

An example of the use of advertising in the press to promote peace was the campaign organised by Women Strike for Peace through the *New York Times* of 1 June 1980. The main headlines were:

A MESSAGE TO THE LEADERS OF NUCLEAR WEAPONS
WE DO NOT WANT OUR CHILDREN TO BE THE LAST
GENERATION

The advert included a cut-off slip which the reader could cut out, putting in his name and address, to send to President Carter, The White House, Washington DC, to express support for Proposition 1 in relation to efforts to get the major powers to seek agreement on nuclear disarmament.

*Black picketing a Washington bank to protest at having to use a side window rather than the main entrance*

**Larzac** Larzac plateau in Southern France was an important sheep-farming area. In October 1970 the government decided on a huge extension of the existing military camp on the plateau. This would destroy the existing community, causing some 58 farms to close down, with 40 others being seriously affected.

The local people formed an Association in 1971 to protect their interests and their campaign to oppose the government's plan gained wide support abroad from groups concerned about human rights, conservation, peace or lifestyles. Despite an effective campaign of obstruction and civil disobedience over many years, success was only achieved in 1981, when the new President, François Mitterrand, cancelled the extension project.

**Civil disobedience**   This involves not only non-violent opposition but refusal to obey what are considered unjust laws. This method was used by Gandhi and others in South Africa, by Gandhi in India and the French farmers in Larzac, to mention a few examples. When a government prosecutes offenders, it is often seen as cruel and oppressive, and public opinion may eventually force the government to make reforms.

**Gandhi's form of civil disobedience**   Mohandas Gandhi qualified as a barrister in Britain and afterwards campaigned against unjust race laws in South Africa before returning to his native land, India. He abandoned western lifestyle in favour of living simply, dressed only in a loin-cloth, white shawl and sandals. This impressed many of the poor who called him Mahatma ('great soul').

Gandhi led the campaign for independence from Britain. His method of civil disobedience he called *Satyagraha* ('truth-force') based on his beliefs in *satya* (truth), *ahimsa* (non-violence) and *tapasya* (readiness to suffer injury rather than to inflict it) as a means of influencing his opponents. In March 1930 he led a march to Dandi on the coast where he and his followers made salt, which is necessary to keep healthy in a hot country like India, by boiling sea water. His demonstration was against the high tax on salt and the fact that the British government alone was allowed to produce it.

*A demonstration in 1966 against the Vietnam War*

# ACTIVITIES

1. Which one of the following has been associated with a campaign by women against the siting of Pershing and Cruise missiles in Britain?
(a) Burnham Common  (b) Clapham Common  (c) Greenham Common
(d) Farnham Common. Do you think such campaigning can help reduce the threat of war?

2. Find out how Lord Baden-Powell of Gilwell, once the youngest general in the British Army, was able to adapt certain military virtues and skills for the cause of peace through the Boy Scout Movement, founded in 1907.

3. Suggest a relationship between the saying by John Donne 'No man is an island' and the idea contained in Genesis 4 : 9.

4. Matching question:
Do a research project to discover some of the important people and organisations involved in humanitarian and peace work or the struggle for justice over the last 300 years. In particular find out information about the organisations and people mentioned below and match the details on the left with the correct name listed on the right.

(a) Leader of a lengthy strike of Californian grape pickers

George Fox (1624–91)

(b) Gained Nobel Peace Prize (1906), author of *Twenty Years at Hull House*

Emmeline Pankhurst

(c) Spiritual father of the work-camp movement and founder of International Voluntary Service for Peace

David Thompson

(d) Founder of the Society of Friends (Quakers)

Jane Addams

(e) Born in Norwich and worked to make prisons and convict ships more humane

Mother Theresa

(f) Committee of 100

Martin Luther King

(g) Peace Pledge Union

John Wesley

(h) European Movement for Disarmament (END)

John Collins

(i) Founder of Methodism who worked for social reform

Elisabeth Fry (1780–1845)

(j) Worked in India and founded an International Association of volunteers to help the very poor

Pierre Ceresole (1874–1945)

(k) First Chairman of the Campaign for Nuclear Disarmament

Bertrand Russell

(l) Baptist pastor from Alabama, who campaigned against racial segregation and for Civil Rights in the USA

David Sheppard (1880–1937)

(m) The Suffragettes

Cesar Chavez

5.	Study the *Daily Telegraph*, *The Times* or *The Guardian* over a week and collect or make a note of the headlines and details of ten articles relating to the activities of groups covering to one of the following:	(a) peace	(b) the environment	(c) the Third World.

6.	Find out more details about	(a) the Larzac affair	(b) Gandhi's career and work. (Information is available in the series of sheets 'Grassroots in Action' available from the Peace Pledge Union, 6 Endsleigh Street, London WC1.)

7.	Devise a version of a snakes and ladders game, using ladders for things which might help promote a peaceful society and snakes for things which are likely to contribute to a more violent and unpeaceful society.

---

# 7.3 Crime Prevention and Alternatives to Aggression

## Ways of Reducing Crime and Violence in Society

Just as people differ in their views about the reasons for violence and crime (discussed in Chapter 1), so there are differences of opinion over the remedies. Probably some combination of all the four main proposals outlined below would achieve some success.

1. **Strengthen deterrents**	People who tend to place the blame on the individual for the growth of crime and violence in society are also inclined to support the need for strong deterrents. These include tighter or stronger laws, harsher punishments including longer jail sentences, capital punishment for certain crimes, possibly hard labour on public works, for example road building, and a stronger, better equipped police force.

2. **Introduce reforms**	Some argue that unjust laws, government policies and the actions of powerful individuals or organisations which oppress or manipulate others may be responsible for part of any growth in violence and crime. Efforts should be made to identify and remedy any grievances which helped cause crime. Reforms would include new laws which protect the weak and poor, better working and living conditions, removal of forms of discrimination, greater employment opportunities.

3. **Encourage vigilance**	This approach involves greater co-operation between the police and the public based on the theme 'Let's beat crime together'. The majority of crimes affecting the public are burglaries, crimes involving cars and vandalism, and these are hard to prevent and detect. Local

police authorities in Britain have introduced neighbourhood watch or crime prevention schemes, with suggestions on preventing crime and protecting property/possessions, and what to do if you see anything suspicious.

**4.  Discover constructive outlets**  These include various forms of recreational, artistic and sporting activities which improve the mind and body, or work of a voluntary or social service nature which helps others.

# Role of the Citizen in Keeping the Law

Frequently people stress their rights rather than their duties or responsibilities as tax-paying citizens of a country. They expect the police to help and protect them in need, but are not always so anxious to co-operate with the police in preventing or solving crime. Instead they rely on someone else to get involved, or believe that it is only the job of the police. This is known as 'passing the buck', illustrated in the cartoon below. Once an American professor staged a series of 250 mock break-ins by his students. About 8000 people witnessed the incidents, but only 12 tried to stop the fake robbers. Investigations carried out in the Paris Metro have found that people were reluctant to help individuals who were being assaulted.

If an individual is attacked it is lawful for him or her to use such force as is necessary for self-defence to ward off the attacker. In addition, that person should be prepared to go to the aid of someone else who is attacked. As it is our duty to keep the law, a citizen can arrest anyone breaking the law. This is known as a citizen's arrest.

**Vigilantism**   Understandably the government and police discourage the public from 'taking the law into its own hands', as this can result in anarchy, and possibly greater injustice.

The American frontiersman thought that violence in self-defence was justified, but this developed into vigilantism and 'lynch law'. Even today some individuals or mobs may take personal revenge for criminal acts if they think the government and police have not provided adequate protection or if there has been an unjust decision made by the courts of law. The actors Charles Bronson and Arnold Schwarzenegger have shown this approach as the self-elected dispensers of justice in the films *Death Wish IV* and *Commando*.

**Role of the police**   The distinction between soldiers and the police is a comparatively modern one. The enforcement of law, maintenance of order and the protection of the innocent, which today is regarded as police work, was until relatively recent times the work of soldiers. Even today there are situations such as the present troubles in Northern Ireland where the army supplements the work of the police.

---

Social scientists differ over whether man's aggressiveness is inherited or learned, but they do agree that it can be modified. 'When angered,' wrote one, 'a 17th century nobleman might automatically reach for his sword, a 19th century cowboy for his gun and a 20th century Englishman for a pen so that he could write a letter to the London Times.'

Some primitive communities employ similar institutions to channel hostilities.

Some Eskimos, for example, regulate conflicts in a kind of duel in which each party sings sarcastic songs about the other, with the spectators deciding the winner. And Indians on the west coast of Canada practise the custom of giving an opponent large quantities of blankets, horses, oil and other possessions, thus shaming him with a loss of status until he can do likewise.

'The white man fights with his hands,' said one chief, 'but we fight with property.'

The white man – or any civilised man, for that matter – does not always fight, however. According to sociologist Harry Holbert Turney-High, man has many outlets for aggression – sex, narcotics, witchcraft, the fine arts and religion as well as violence.

More specifically, he writes, man can release his aggressions by watching a bullfight or smoking a cigarette or celebrating Halloween or cracking a dirty joke or watching a play or saying a prayer.

*Extract from 'Taming a "Savage Beast"', Los Angeles Times, 16 April 1972*

---

# Why do People Like Violence in Films?

On seeing the film *Straw Dogs* the writer says:

'Inside the cinema I sat in front of two middle-aged ladies who waded through boxes of Bassett's liquorice allsorts and packets of cigarettes, screwing themselves up, screaming, breathless with excitement and fear. When Susan George hesitated with the shot gun, one of them shouted: 'Shoot!' which she did to a chorus of 'Well done!' When Dustin Hoffman finally pulled himself together and got violent and someone's foot was blown off, the ladies behind applauded vigorously, as did many of the audience.'

As an answer to why people enjoy violent films, Dr Robert Shields, *The Observer*'s psychology correspondent, exclaims:

'For many people, especially the young, there's always an impulse to experience what's both dangerous or at the extremes of feeling. Riding a motorbike at 100 mph – where the individual is getting as near to death as he can, but avoiding it. So, in violent films, the notion of actually seeing what the worst is like, horrific events, is to some very fascinating.'

*Extracts from John Heilpern 'Ultra Violence/The New Wave',* The Observer, *23 January 1972*

**"116 . . . 117 . . . 118 dead!! Pass it on."**

Daily Express, *20 June 1972*

1. What would you do if you saw someone committing some minor crime, such as shoplifting?

2. Suggest some four common sense precautions which can be taken to prevent **(a)** attack while walking home late at night in a large town   **(b)** theft in your home while on holiday.

3. A clue to the role of the citizen regarding law and order can be found in the Bible in Romans 12: 17–21 and 13: 1–7. Would you regard these two passages as conflicting or complementary?

4. In groups discuss the extract 'What Can Parents Do?' below. Imagine that each of you were parents and answer the following questions.

   **(a)** What do you think of the five suggestions? Could they be worded better? Would you delete any points or add others?

   **(b)** As a group compose the words of a short talk a parent might give his son to discourage him from shoplifting.

   ### WHAT CAN PARENTS DO?

   1   Talk to the youngsters. Explain that shoplifting is a crime and that a criminal record is a lifelong shadow.

   2   Emphasize that going along with the crowd for fear of being 'chicken' is the coward's way out.

   3   When youngsters go on group shopping expeditions, know how much money your son or daughter has, where the group is going, what they expect to buy.

   4   If your son or daughter comes home with more merchandise than he or she has money to buy, ask about it. And don't take easy answers about where it came from. Sales slips are a proof of purchase.

   5   Outlaw all clothes swapping unless the parents on both sides know what's being exchanged.

   *Queensland Police Department*

5. Answer the following questions on the extract 'Taming a "Savage Beast"'.

   **(a)** Which word in the text is associated with a common method used until the 19th century of settling disputes between gentlemen?

   **(b)** What examples given of alternatives to aggression or violent acts might be **(i)** considered forms of relaxation   **(ii)** the turning of conflict into ritual?

   **(c)** Explain clearly the meaning of the following: 'loss of status'; 'fine arts'; Halloween.

6. Explain Jesus' attitude to violence. Refer to Matthew 5: 38–48; Luke 6: 27–36; Matthew 26: 50–2; John 18: 2–11.

7. Work out how the term 'violence' is thought of in the Old Testament. Refer, for example, to Micah 6: 12; Jeremiah 22: 13–17; Psalm 72; Ezekiel 45: 9.

8. What can be done by the following groups to discourage anti-social activities (violence, vandalism and indiscipline) in certain schools and in the local community?
(a) parents  (b) pupils  (c) teachers  (d) local councillors.

9. In small groups make suggestions for a possible Do's and Don'ts code which might apply for everyone at home, in a classroom, or on a cross-channel ferry.

10. The Giles cartoon on page 125 (*Daily Express*) is based on the crash of an airplane in which all 118 passengers and crew are killed. The crowds of sightseers stopped the emergency services reaching the scene quickly.  (a) Why are the people made to look like sheep? (b) What is Giles trying to illustrate in the drawing?

11. Answer the questions below based on the extract which follows:

> 'The shari'a code, with its Old-Testament principle of an eye for an eye, is common to all forms of Islam . . . the value of punishment as a deterrent is almost universally accepted in the Moslem world . . . Why, they ask, should we adopt western liberal laws and reformist penology if they lead to the murders, muggings and drug scandals of London and New York?'

The Economist, *16 July 1977*

(a) Which method of preventing crime suggested on pages 122–3 is supported by the Sharia code?

(b) Find the text in the Old Testament from which the 'eye for an eye' philosophy derives.

(c) Would you regard this idea as relevant to certain situations today in your community or in the world generally?

(d) What sort of deterrents have been used in recent times in Saudi Arabia and Pakistan to deter crime? Why are such punishments rarely used in the West?

12. Choose a representative from your class or group to contact the local police station to find out details from its Community Service or Crime Prevention Department on the following:  (a) the role of the police  (b) crime prevention.

13. Have a class discussion on the following:  (a) what it means to be a good sport
(b) virtues of competitive team sports versus individual sports like mountaineering
(c) circumstances when sport can be a healthy alternative to aggression or violence (whether for players or spectators) and when it might encourage aggression.

# 8 RELIGIONS AND CULTURES

## 8.1  Peace and Forms of Conflict in Religion

### Christianity and Other Religions

In 1980 the size of the adult memberships of non-Christian religious groups in Britain was led by the Muslims (600 000), Sikhs (150 000), Jews (110 915), Hindus (110 000). Elsewhere in the world, even if Christians are a large minority, the main religion or belief is either Hindu or Buddhist, Jewish or Islamic, Marxist or secular.

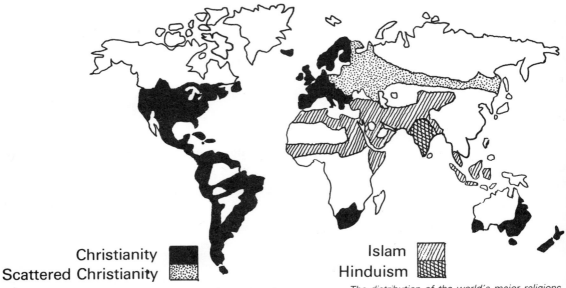

Christianity ■
Scattered Christianity ▒

Islam ▨
Hinduism ▦

*The distribution of the world's major religions*

Life would be boring if everybody thought in the same way or had similar customs and ways of life. Various differences between people can be a means of unity rather than division, as each of us learns to appreciate and enjoy some aspects of the way of life and cultures of other countries.

Various factors such as age, culture, position, previous experience or expectations cause each of us to see the same object, event or situation differently.

Some people, like the followers of Jainism, believe that it is stupid or futile to fight others because of deep differences of religious, cultural or political beliefs. As the famous parable of the blind men and the elephant teaches, everyone sees truth from a different angle, so it is pointless to kill someone because you disagree.

---

## THE ELEPHANT

There were six blind people. They heard that the king was visiting the next village, riding on an elephant. None of them had ever seen an elephant. 'An elephant!' they said. 'I wonder what an elephant is like.'

They went to find out. Each of them went alone. The first held the elephant's trunk. The second, a tusk. The third, an ear. The fourth, a leg. The fifth, the stomach. The sixth, the tail. Then they went home, all sure that they now knew exactly what the elephant looked like.

They began to tell each other. 'Oh it's a fantastic elephant', said the first, 'so slow and soft, long and strong.' 'No', said the one who had felt the tusk. 'It's quite short, and very hard.' 'You're both of you wrong', said the third, who had felt the ear. 'The elephant is flat and thin like a big leaf.' 'Oh no,' said the fourth, who had felt the leg, 'It's like a tree.'

And the other two joined in too – 'It's like a wall', 'it's like a rope.' They argued and argued, and their argument grew very bitter. They began to fight.

Then someone came up who could see. 'You are all right', said this person who could see. 'All the parts together are the elephant.'

---

Various approaches to better understanding and improved world relationships can in a sense be considered as elephants. Thus some studies in secondary schools, variously labelled as shown in the diagram below, all have the same broad aims even though the approach and emphasis will differ.

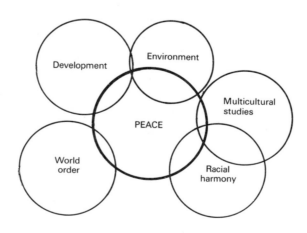

It is not true that other religions are all darkness. They are full of light of which Jesus Christ is both the author and fulfilment, and it is necessary for us to approach other religions with a great reverence for them, as well as with our belief in Jesus as Himself the word, the light, the perfect image.

*Archbishop Ramsey*

All men are the leaves and fruit of one same tree . . . they all have the same origin. The same rain has fallen upon them all, the same sun makes them grow, they are all refreshed by the same breeze . . . the whole of humanity is enveloped by the Mercy and Grace of God.

*Abdu'l-Bahá*

## REVERENCE FOR OTHER FAITHS

All faiths constitute a revelation of Truth, but all are imperfect, and liable to error. Reverence for other faiths need not blind us to their faults. We must be keenly alive to the defects of our own faith also, yet not leave it on that account, but try to overcome those defects. Hence the necessity of tolerance which does not mean indifference to one's own faith, but a more intelligent and purer love for it.

*Mahatma Gandhi*

## JONAH AND PEACE

The story of Jonah in the Old Testament of the Bible teaches us that God cares for, and forgives, people of different cultures and faiths. The dove is a peace symbol and in Hebrew Jonah means 'dove'. One movement is called Jews Organised for a Nuclear Arms Halt (Jonah).

**Purpose in Life**   Some argue that each of us needs to believe in a religion since this helps us distinguish between good and evil. Without a religious faith, there is no deterrent apart from the law to prevent us from committing anti-social or immoral acts. Others would argue that many religious people have committed acts in the past, and continue to do so today, which they regard as unjust and immoral and that many of no faith at all lead more honest and praiseworthy lives than religious people.

Some people wonder whether humanity is capable of solving the numerous problems facing the world without a strong or firm belief in God. Gandhi and others have felt that successful non-violent resistance would necessitate such a belief. However, many agnostics or atheists with concern for the importance of moral or ethical values belong to peace movements and usually have a strong belief in the importance of the good triumphing over all that is bad, the basic unity of all people and the intrinsic worth of all human beings.

**Prayer** In the sixth chapter of his letter to the Ephesians, St Paul said that we are involved in spiritual warfare with the powers that be. Some people see prayer as a means of reclaiming our identity as the 'children of God' and helps us regain ourselves from the control of technologies, institutions and assumptions that could lead us to destruction. Historically, prayer and worship have always been at the heart of the strongest expressions of Christian witness against tyranny and violence. Religious people believe that prayer helps to humble us and to transform us individually into better people. Prayer is not a substitute for action, they maintain, but the basis for all the other actions we take. Religious people pray for various reasons. This includes the need to thank, ask, obtain/request forgiveness, praise or express pleasure.

---

A methodist minister visiting a prison said to some of the hardened criminals: 'You are not really men until you have learnt to pray.'

---

Father Fynn sj used to tell the story in his retreat lectures of the ship, rudderless and adrift off the east coast of South America. Water had run out and all on board thought they were lost. A ship came into view. 'Give us water!', they semaphored to their saviours. 'Put down a bucket where you are!', was signalled back. So they did and behold fresh water miles out to sea! It seems that the Amazon is so powerful that, miles out from its mouth the water is still fresh.

*Graham English and friends*, Horraymus, *1983*

---

Peace cannot be built by the power of rulers alone. Peace can be firmly constructed only if it corresponds to the absolute determination of all people of good will. Rulers must be supported by and enlightened by a public opinion that encourages them or, where necessary, expresses disapproval.

*From Pope John Paul's 1982 Peace Day Message*

## PRAYER FOR PEACE

Lead me from Death to Life
from Falsehood to Truth
Lead me from Despair to Hope
from Fear to Trust
Lead me from Hate to Love
from War to Peace
Let Peace fill our Heart
our World, our Universe
Peace Peace Peace

*This prayer began to circulate in England in 1981. Its source is not clear but its appeal is not confined to members of religions.*

Lord make me an instrument of your PEACE
Where there is hatred, let me sow love.
Where there is injury, pardon.
Where there is doubt, faith.
Where there is despair, hope.

*St Francis of Assisi*

**Compassion and caring**  A fundamental tenet of much religious and moral teaching is that if people worked for the good of others, they would also benefit themselves.

'the real way to get happiness is by giving out happiness to other people'.

*Lord Baden-Powell*

A man had died and was about to enter heaven. First he requested to discover what hell was like. He was shown a large hall where a sumptuous meal was displayed on a long table. Around this sat various skeletons. Only three foot long chopsticks were available with which to eat. Later the man found to his surprise that the same scene existed in heaven except that this time the people looked extremely well-fed, even though they too only had three foot long chopsticks. He asked why the people looked so healthy compared to the occupants of hell. His guide smiled and pointed out that in hell the people had starved, only being prepared to help themselves, whereas in heaven the people had thrived as they had helped each other.

## OR NOT AT ALL?

In all lost souls
Do you see yourself
In all heartache
And fallen pride,
Do you feel forgiving,
Crying, compassionate,
Or not at all?

In all weakness
What do you reflect;
In all searching
And hope that fails,
Where do you find yourself
Caring, considering,
Or not at all?

*Philip Barker*

---

Please put Your divine foot down and order a little more restraint and common sense among Your believers. Tell them to stop fighting one another with all the ferocity and wickedness at their command and blaming it on You. Make it clear that they must bear the responsibility for their own misdeeds and cannot commit endless evil, including mass-murder, in Your name (as given in their various Holy Scriptures).

*Material adapted or quoted from George Mikes,* How to be God, *1984*

---

## IMAGES OF PEACE

Possessions are positively dangerous because they often encourage unconcern for the poor, because they lead to strife and war, and because they seduce people into forsaking God.

*Ronald J Sider,* Rich Christians in an Age of Hunger, *1979*

---

## WHO ARE THE PEOPLE OF PEACE?

justice-people who cry out
against the oppressors of people,
the destroyers of the earth,
those who would bomb and burn and obliterate;

nurture-people who grow plants and feed birds
and pick up dirt from the earth
and love what is green, fresh and growing;

healing-people whose hands touch others
into life and well-being,
struggling always against the forces of death;

fun-people who lift up and lighten
and laugh others into fruitfulness
and courage for the long haul;

young-people who have nothing to gain
by destruction and death but death itself;

little-people who don't know themselves as special
but who are in truth the 'salt of the earth',
feeding and clothing and housing the human family
from one end of day to the next.

*From a poem by Jane Blewett, published in the newsletter of Center Focus, Center.for Concern, Washington DC*

## Pacifism

Pacifists believe that the abolition of war is both desirable and possible. Pacifism in the strict sense of an unconditional renunciation of war by an individual is, so far as we know, a little less than 2000 years old, traceable to the Roman world.

The early Christian church was predominantly pacifist, believing war and killing to be contrary to the way of Jesus. As Christians gained more influence, and especially with the accession of Constantine as Emperor of the Roman Empire in the early 4th century, the church came to accept the need for armed force in the 'Christianised' empire.

Since then mainstream Christianity has accepted armed force as necessary for the defence of justice and right and, indeed, Christians have fought on opposite sides of the same wars. (See the 'just war' theory, Chapter 5.) However, there has always been a small minority who maintained the pacifist position, such as the Anabaptists in the 16th century, the Mennonites, the Society of Friends (Quakers), the Church of the Brethren and the Kimbanguist Church of the Congo (Zaire). In addition there are minority pacifist groups within the larger Christian denominations.

For most pacifists their faith begins with a sense of the oneness of the human family and the sanctity of human life. For Christians there is the special unity of the Christian family, the 'body of Christ', in St Paul's phrase, and for them the deliberate killing of other humans is both a crime against humanity and a sin against God. Christ's teaching on human relationships centres on love as a positive, sacrificial dedication to the service of others. To Christian pacifists this also means using love as a method in human relationships, a means of changing things and people.

An important principle acceptable to Christian and non-Christian pacifists, Buddhists, Jainists and others occurs in Christ's Sermon on the Mount (Matthew 5: 38–47). This states that evil cannot be overcome by evil, only by non-resistance and good.

The death of Christ on the cross is regarded by some as the supreme example of this. Whether Christian or not, at the heart of the pacifist faith is the view that in human relationships the results you get tend to be of the same nature as the methods you use. Violence and hatred lead to further violence and hatred. The only way to break the chain is by introducing their opposites, since love can lead to reconciliation.

Declaration of Principles of the Non-resistance Society (1838) as quoted in *The Pacifist Conscience*, includes the extract:

We are bound by the laws of a Kingdom which is not of this world; the subjects of which are forbidden to fight . . . Our country is the world, our countrymen are all mankind.

*Peter Mayer, 1966*

**Religion and social responsibility** Some people say that the church should not concern itself with politics but only with spiritual matters. Others argue that politics should not be narrowly interpreted as concerned with government and elections but that it involves the whole life of a community and its problems, and that evangelicalism (defending and spreading the Christian faith) should be linked with social action. An extreme form of this view is known as liberation theology, a belief adopted especially by some priests in the Third World, entailing the use of political activity as a means of achieving social reform.

Evangelism and social action are: 'Like the two blades of a pair of scissors or two wings of a bird.'

*Grand Rapids Report, Church Evangelicalists, 1982*

I have a strong conviction that you cannot properly serve God unless you endeavour to the best of your ability to serve man in community.

*Canon John Collins*

On 28 August 1963 the Reverend Martin Luther King (1929–68) led a march to Washington DC, and there he shared his dream of a multi-racial America.

### HATE CANNOT DRIVE OUT HATE, ONLY LOVE CAN DO THAT

I have a dream . . .
that one day on the red hills of Georgia
the sons of former slaves
and the sons of former slave-owners
will be able to sit down together
at the table of brotherhood.
I have a dream . . .
that my four little children
will one day live in a nation
where they will not be judged
by the colour of their skins
but by the content of their character.

*Martin Luther King*

## ACTIVITIES

1. Rearrange the items on the right-hand side of the following list so that they pair up with their equivalents on the left.

   (a) Man is made by his beliefs. As he believes, so he is.
   *Bhagarad Gita*                                          Christian Scientists

   (b) Motto is 'Blood and Fire'.                           Buddhism

   (c) Mary Baker Eddy.                                     Sikhism

   (d) Believers face Mecca to pray.                        Bahá'í Faith

   (e) Banyan or fig tree.                                  Hinduism

   (f) Singh (lion).                                        Salvation Army

   (g) 'My heart was strangely warmed'
   *John Wesley, 22 May 1738*                               Islam

   (h) Ahimsa (non-violence).                               Methodism

   (i) Belief in unifying the world's religions as a
   means to attain world peace.                             Jainism

2. Suggest three ways you can take more care of, or care about (a) yourself (b) members of your family (c) others (d) the environment.

3. What is the word used in the Bible (occurring 19 times in the New Testament) which warns of the dangers of riches?

4. Find out details about the life and importance of St Francis of Assisi. Write your own poem or prayer about caring and peace.

5. Find extracts in the New Testament which deal with caring, overcoming selfishness and narrow-mindedness, being assertive in a good cause, and the notion of faith, hope and charity (or love). For example, refer to the following: Romans 8:31; Mark 10:45; Romans 2:15; Beatitudes, Matthew 5:1–12; I Corinthians 13:1–13.

6. List all the faiths and denominations of Christianity in your area. Select one faith and one denomination each, as part of a group activity. By means of interviews find out why and when it was formed, and after study research make a table listing the main aspects of each faith or denomination.

7. 'Blessed are the peacemakers for they shall be called Sons of God.'

*Matthew 5:9.*

(a) avoids conflicts (b) easy-going and relaxed (c) peace at any price (d) settle quarrels, but does not start them (e) tolerant and not negative (f) compromises convictions when pressured by others (g) feels internally at ease.

Arrange the above in order starting with the one which best conforms to your idea of a peacemaker and finish with the one which least conforms.

8. Find out how the following terms are generally understood: a religion, faith, cult, sect, denomination, pagan, fringe religion, non-conformist.

9. Find out the religions that relate to each of the symbols below.

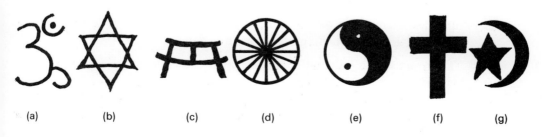

(a)    (b)    (c)    (d)    (e)    (f)    (g)

10. Find out details about the Yoga and meditation (body-mind training) and their links with religions such as Hinduism. How might Yoga help a person understand his or her inner or real self?

11. How did Jesus react to conflict? Read Leviticus 23:3, then compare with Mark 2:23–8; Matthew 12:1–15; Mark 3:1–16; Luke 6:6–11; Luke 22:47–53.

12. Prepare a case study on the life and work of Martin Luther King. Mention his position on the subject of liberation theology.

# 8.2 Appreciating Other Cultures and Life Styles

What seems reasonable, normal or self-evident in one country or culture may be viewed in a quite different light by someone from a different country or cultural background, whether this refers to attitudes, behaviour, customs or laws. For example, in the United States and Britain a common way to call a waiter is to point upward with the forefinger, whereas in Asia such an act is reserved to call a dog or other animal. In Africa, one knocks on the table to call a waiter.

In Western and Arab cultures lengthy eye contact with a person is acceptable, whereas in Japan such behaviour is considered rude, and the Japanese focus instead on a person's neck or tie knot.

In the West it is usually considered rude to be late for appointments whereas in Arab countries lateness is not regarded in the same way.

In African circles the family includes both the immediate family and the extended family or tribe. The old are cared for by the family whereas in the West it is not considered unnatural to send elderly relatives to institutions.

A Frenchman may have bread with each meal and often dips his bread into a beverage when eating. This practice might be considered bad manners by certain people in Britain.

In Islamic countries the left hand is considered to be the toilet hand and so is never used for touching others as in a handshake.

There may also be conflict between two principles: the respect for other cultures on the one hand and the desire to adhere to certain specific principles on the other. Muslims, for example, may not want their family 'contaminated', as they might see it, by materialistic and secular Western values.

# Destroyed . . . by a hunger to live

AS wintry gales blow across Europe it's an appropriate moment for Channel 4 to revive its 1984 series **Survive,** if only to demonstrate that, weatherwise things could be a whole lot worse.

The Frozen North, first of six programmes on the theme of endurance in the face of almost certain death, directed its main attention to the case of a quiet, decent Canadian 'bush pilot' who, even all other hope was gone, clung to life only by eating the flesh of a fellow human.

The pilot's subsequent notoriety, fuelled by lurid accounts of his ordeal published and broadcast by the Canadian and world media, convinced him that death, even starvation, would be preferable to the hysteria of the professional headline-hunters.

The pilot's name is Marten Hartwell. In the mid-winter of 1972 he took off in his single-engined aircraft to fly a nurse and two Eskimo patients to a hospital in the Canadian Arctic.

The plane crashed in a remote, snowbound, forested area. Two of the passengers – the nurse and a pregnant woman – died within hours, leaving the pilot with both legs broken, and a teenage Eskimo boy named David, who survived for 24 days.

Before he died, the Eskimo lad was asked by Hartwell whether he would eat human flesh, since they had now exhausted their few rations and faced sure starvation. The boy replied: 'Shut up. I am goint to die now.' David died that night.

Unable to crawl away from the scene on his scattered limbs, Hartwell shouted his defiance to the uncaring skies: 'I could not believe that there was a God who wouldn't help me out of this situation if I didn't help myself . . . Then I started eating . . . it was the beginning of my survival . . . the worse thing was taking the first bit.'

A little over a week later he was rescued by a helicopter crew after the longest air hunt in Canadian history. Hartwell pleaded with his rescuers not to tell reporters about his cannibalism, but his trust was betrayed. He was Big News. The headlines may be imagined. 'Here,' he said, 'the horror started.' Hartwell was recognised everywhere, hounded by curious stares, an object of curiosity and revulsion.

What, he was asked in last night's programme, would he do if it were to happen again? He replied: 'I would stretch out and say "I am going to die now . . ."'

Because of the cannibalism? 'No,' Hartwell replied, 'because of the Press reaction, because of the publicity.'

When he was rescued Hartwell was dark-haired and apparently healthy. Now, a decade later, he was grey and gaunt. He'had eaten flesh because he wanted to live. Later he was himself, devoured by men who were hungry only for a good story.

Daily Mail, *4 February 1986*

# ACTIVITIES

1. In the past, and in some remote communities today, some cultures or groups practise cannibalism. Answer the following based on the extract from the *Daily Mail*.

   (a) Despite the fact that people frequently harm and kill others, most people have strong inhibitions about eating their own kind. Are these inhibitions justified?

   (b) Are there certain situations, as for example the one described in this extract, when a person is justified in resorting to cannibalism?

   (c) Does the extract seem to imply from Hartwell's cry of defiance to the uncaring skies that God only helps those who help themselves?

   (d) Explain what is meant by 'professional headline-hunters'.

2. Write a brief essay on cultural habits and traditions based on personal experiences or those drawn from the local neighbourhood. Refer, if necessary, to some of the following: (a) relationships within the family (b) religious practices and festivals (c) food differences and methods of eating/preparation (d) music and dancing (e) styles of architecture (f) living styles in houses (g) forms of dress, hairstyles or head gear.

3. Imagine you and your family have to live for ten years among people in a country where the religion, the culture, and thus the values, are very different to your own. How do you think you would cope? Would you try to change your views and customs to theirs?

# 9 REVISIONIST VIEWS ON THE COLD WAR AND UNILATERALISM

## Introduction

This chapter is very largely the counterpart of Chapter 6, presenting an alternative or opposing viewpoint concerning the Cold War, the arms race, and the role and importance of nuclear weapons. Some of the arguments used by unilateralists and supporters of the non-use of nuclear weapons under any circumstances are covered here. Note that unilateralists are not necessarily opposed to the use of conventional weapons in defence, but since the use of conventional weapons can escalate a war into a nuclear conflict, many unilateralists support social defence, recommended by the opponents of physical violence and discussed on pages 118–20, and previously mentioned in Chapter 5, page 87.

## 9.1   Revisionist Views of the Cold War

The causes of the Cold War, as seen by many people in the West, are discussed in Chapter 6. The arguments put forward by the Russians justifying their point of view were largely ignored until the 1960s. Then a number of left-wing historians in the United States and elsewhere developed an alternative view of the causes and progress of the Cold War since 1945, which was more sympathetic towards the Soviet position.

While 'hardliners' in the West, or extreme right-wingers, tend to place all the blame for the start of the Cold War on the USSR, and extreme anti-Americans in the Soviet Union put all the blame on the USA, others take a more moderate view and realise that both sides are partly to blame. However, below is a point of view favourable to the Russian position which totally ignores the Western arguments, just as the extract on page 92, Chapter 6, ignored the Russian view.

## THE RUSSIAN VIEW

The blame for the Cold War lies entirely with the 'capitalist' Western powers, notably the United States. The West has been hostile towards Russia since the communist revolution of 1917. The USA only recognised the new Soviet state in 1933, while during the Second World War the American government failed to give us detailed information about the development of the atomic bomb and its use against Japan. Further, the USA seemed determined to preserve exclusive control of this terrible weapon as shown by the Baruch Plan presented to the United Nations in 1945.

After the death of President Roosevelt on 12 April 1945, the new President, Harry Truman, was difficult to deal with in post-war negotiations. After the dropping of the atomic bomb and the Baruch proposal, the USSR was particularly determined that the corrupting influence of Western ideas hostile to the real interests of ordinary people would not penetrate the East. In any case, the spread of Soviet influence throughout Eastern Europe was legitimate for many reasons. Firstly, we wanted to build a 'cordon sanitaire' as a security measure to prevent further invasions of Russia from the West, as had occurred in 1812 (with Napoleon Bonaparte), 1918–21 (Allied intervention in support of the 'white' armies), and 1941 (German invasion). Secondly, in the Stalin–Churchill 'percentages' agreement of October 1944, it had been agreed that the USSR would have preponderant influence in certain Eastern European countries and a shared influence with Britain in Greece. The USA persistently refused to recognise the validity of this arrangement. Thirdly, the USA ignored the assumption underlying the agreements at Yalta and Potsdam that governments in Eastern Europe after 1945 must be friendly with the USSR. If Western-style 'bourgeois' elections had been held this would have resulted in the growth of influence of capitalists (industrialists and landowners) so that these countries would have followed anti-Soviet policies.

A Russian view from the satirical magazine, Krokodil, of the Western allies hatching a new Nazi Germany

The extraction of heavy reparations from Germany from 1945 was necessary as compensation for the heavy war-time losses suffered in men and resources (far greater than those suffered by the USA and Britain). The USSR also had good reason to distrust the USA which refused to allow the Russians any share in the Allied military occupation of Japan in 1945, and took the hostile act of constructing a series of military bases which ringed the USSR, such as at Okinawa (Japan). Naturally the USSR has tried to counter this hostile act by gaining allies outside this ring. The USSR has obtained bases in strategic locations so that it can adequately protect itself in a nuclear war, and to counter the growth of hostile alliances such as Nato and Seato.

142

## THE FREEZE

Many people say, 'The Freeze is a good idea, but what about the Russians?' These are some of the questions people are asking about the Russians:

Can we trust them?

- to adopt our view of the world? No. The Russians will go on supporting people we oppose and running their country in ways we don't like. The Freeze will not end our political differences. But it will lessen the chance that we'll blow ourselves up over those differences.

- to agree to a nuclear weapons Freeze? Possibly. We won't know until we propose it to them. We do know that they have expressed interest in the idea several times. The Freeze is in their best interest – and in ours. Our job is to get enough officials on both sides to understand that fact.

- to stick by a freeze agreement? Based on their record, yes. The US and USSR have signed many nuclear arms control agreements, including major treaties such as SALT and the 1963 Limited Test Ban.

Some people say the Russians would have no incentive for arms control if we weren't threatening them by building more weapons. In fact the Russians have their own reasons for stopping the nuclear arms race – the same reasons we have. The Freeze will improve the national security of both countries by reducing the military threat they pose to each other, and by enabling their economies to better serve the needs of their people.

Here are some of the reasons the Freeze is in the Russian interest:

**1.** They will be less secure if the nuclear arms race continues. A Freeze now will stop the move to first-strike weapons. The Pershing II missiles scheduled for deployment in Western Europe will be able to reach Russian command posts in six minutes. The MX missile would make Russian land-based missiles more vulnerable than ever.

**2.** They need to improve their economy by spending less money on the arms race. Military spending is more of a burden on the Russian economy than on ours because their Gross National Product is about 40% smaller than ours.

**3.** They don't want to get blown up any more than we do. The Soviet Union lost 20 million people in World War II and had over 70,000 of their villages and cities destroyed.

## DO THE RUSSIANS WANT TO TAKE OVER THE WORLD?

Some people look at Russian actions and see a plan to conquer the world. The Soviet Union has kept control over countries in Eastern Europe and has not allowed free elections there. It has invaded Hungary, Czechoslovakia and Afghanistan. Such actions are to be condemned, as they have been, for the untold suffering they have brought on millions of people.

But do these actions mean that the Russians are out to conquer the world?

Russia has been invaded many times, including three times by the West in this century: during World War I and II by Germany, and in 1919 by the Western allies including the US. From ancient Mongolians to Napoleon to twentieth century Japanese, Russia has suffered at the hands of foreign attack.

Russian history has left a deep-seated fear of invasion, which helps explain why, since World War II, all direct Russian military intervention has taken place along Soviet borders. Today, in a world filled with Cold War tensions, the Russians can take little comfort from the fact that every other country that has nuclear weapons aims them at the Soviet Union.

## ARE THE RUSSIANS GAINING INFLUENCE?

Some believe that the Russian military build-up means more world power for the Soviet Union. Here are the facts:

In recent years the Russians have gained influence in small countries like Ethiopia, Angola and South Yemen. Meanwhile they have lost influence in larger countries like China, India, Egypt and Indonesia.

The high point of Russian influence in the world was in 1958 when pro-Soviet countries accounted for nearly a third of the world's population and a tenth of its economic power. But with the loss of China and other allies, Russian influence today (outside the Soviet Union) covers only 6% of the world's population and one-twentieth of its economic power.

Out of 160 countries in the world today, the Soviet Union has major influence in 19, and none of them are countries of substantial economic or political power. (In contrast, the US, its allies, and other pro-Western countries account for two-thirds of the world's economic, military and political power, according to former CIA analyst Ray Cline.)

*Nuclear Weapons Freeze Campaign*

Did you know?

**1.** In 1977, in article 28 of the new Soviet constitution, the task of universal and complete disarmament was set forth as a major, practical goal of Soviet foreign policy.

**2.** The Russians ran a petition for disarmament before the 1978 UN Special Session that gained 176 million signatures.

*Compiled by Anne Sheikh and Brenda Thomson*

## ACTIVITIES

1. What analogy does the Nuclear Weapons Freeze Campaign use to illustrate that the nuclear arms race is now a 'no-win situation'?

2. What reasons are given in these extracts for the Russian's fear of the West both before and after the Second World War?

3. What reasons are given by the World Disarmament Campaign as to why the Russians are interested in a genuine nuclear weapons freeze?

4. Refer to the extract from Chapter 6, page 92, which gives the American view of the Cold War. Compare this with the Soviet view presented in this section. Using arguments drawn from various parts of this book have a class debate with two speakers defending respectively the American and revisionist view of the Cold War. At the end vote on which side presented the best case.

5. Find out further details about the following mentioned in the revisionist view section: **(a)** reparations **(b)** the Baruch Plan **(c)** the Baghdad Pact **(d)** Allied intervention, 1918–21.

6. Suggest reasons why the Russians feared that Western democracy in Eastern Europe would have led to these countries adopting anti-Soviet policies.

# 9.2 The Case for Unilateral Disarmament and Non-use of Nuclear Weapons

Unilateralists argue that deterrence, the key American and Western strategy to force the Soviet Union to agree to multilateral disarmament, will not necessarily achieve this or guarantee peace. Furthermore it is folly to threaten to use nuclear weapons, whether in attack or defence, when this would result in mutual destruction. Unilateralists argue that a nuclear holocaust could be caused by a number of factors including the following.

**Computer error**   Three times between November 1979 and June 1980, United States nuclear forces were placed on alert because computers showed that North America was about to be attacked by nuclear weapons. If these errors had not been found quickly a nuclear war might have started.

**Accidents**   There have been at least 13 accidents involving aircraft carrying nuclear bombs. Once a B-52 crashed over South Carolina. On recovery it was found that four of the five safety devices (intended to prevent an accident) had been triggered by the fall. Had the bomb exploded, it might have been interpreted as a Russian attack.

**Nature of modern weapons**   The accuracy and small size of modern weapons might tempt an American leader into believing that the West could win a nuclear war if they attacked first. Such weapons include the Trident submarine, the Cruise and MX missiles, and possibly 'Star Wars'.

**Proliferation**   While nuclear weapons exist, knowledge about (and the capacity to produce) nuclear weapons will spread. At the moment about 40 countries have the capacity to produce such weapons while six have already done so, including France, China and India. Nuclear weapons might also fall into the hands of extreme terrorist groups who might have no qualms about using them. Some members of the Non-Proliferation Treaty have violated the treaty for commercial or political benefit. The French have sold reactors to Libya and Iraq, while North Korea and Cuba have received nuclear equipment from the USSR. These developments multiply the risks of nuclear warfare breaking out somewhere.

**Escalation**   A losing side in a conventional war, say Nato forces in Europe, might be tempted to use larger warheads to deter the enemy, and this might lead to the conflict escalating from a local to a world nuclear war.

**Human weakness**   War might start from an incident if a fanatic refused to obey instructions or as a result of human error such as a mistake, a miscalculation or a misunderstanding.

---

President Reagan's idea of a joke has staggered Americans. For he made a spoof announcement that Russia had been outlawed – and would be bombed in five minutes' time.

Presidential aides could hardly believe their ears at the blunder, which happened when technicians asked Mr Reagan to do a voice test before his weekly political broadcast.

He said gravely into the microphone: 'My fellow Americans, I am pleased to tell you we have signed legislation that would outlaw Russia forever.

We begin bombing in five minutes.'

Daily Star, *14 August 1984*

---

*Those whom the gods . . .*

(a lost fragment from *Alice Through the Looking-glass*, with apologies to Lewis Carroll.)

"It is worth it because it works. Forty years of peace. That's what deterrence policy has bought us; forty years of peace!" Humpty Dumpty was almost purple with the excitement of discovering such an argument.

A tiny voice seemed to whisper words like Hungary, Vietnam, Afghanistan, Cambodia, El Salvador, but they meant nothing to Alice now. Her attention was wholly focused on Humpty Dumpty.

"Forty years of peace, there's success for you!"

Alice seemed to recall reading that forty years ago only one nation had an A-bomb. Now six or seven nations had thousands of H-bombs between them. "Yes," she thought, "that's success of a kind." And it occurred to her that forty years ago there were only aircraft to deliver the weapons, then there were rockets, then submarine launchers, then multiple warheads, then . . .

"They make us safe, they give us security", said Humpty Dumpty.

Alice's mind was swimming with confusion and credulity. She half wanted to form a question about accidents and near misses, but the words would not come. Generations of people had given Humpty Dumpty what he wanted, people far wiser than Alice. What arrogance to think that she knew better.

Suddenly, Humpty Dumpty stopped looking into the space above Alice's head, he lowered his eyes and gave her a smile so friendly that she shivered without knowing why.

"And now", he said in a soft voice, "I would like just £300 million more to build an underground headquarters so that if – and of course it will never happen – if there was a war, I could survive to lead you all to victory."

Peace News, *10 December 1982*

## ACTIVITIES

1. Answer the following on the extract from 'Those whom the gods . . .'

   **(a)** In this adaptation of Alice Through the Looking-glass who is Humpty Dumpty meant to be?

   **(b)** What conflicts have occurred in the following places since 1945: Hungary, Vietnam, Afghanistan, Cambodia, El Salvador?

   **(c)** Illustrate how the extract refers to the following: **(i)** proliferation **(ii)** civil defence **(iii)** the nuclear arms race.

   **(d)** Explain in greater detail what is meant by the phrase 'accidents and near misses'.

   **(e)** The title comes from the expression 'Those whom the Gods wish to destroy they first make mad'. What do you think this expression means?

# Attitudes of Young People towards Nuclear Weapons

A study in 1980 by two Harvard psychiatrists involved 1000 elementary and high school students in the United States. Their responses revealed that children felt helpless and uneasy about the future, and that they felt angry about the arrogance of the adults who might blow everyone up.

**British teenagers' thoughts about nuclear war**   More than half the 15- to 18-year-olds in Britain think that there is likely to be a nuclear war in their lifetime. That's the significant outcome of a nationwide survey conducted for *TV Times* in 1983.

| Q What would be the result of Britain abandoning its nuclear weapons? | all % | boys % | girls % |
|---|---|---|---|
| Other countries would follow | 29 | 26 | 32 |
| It would have no effect on other countries' policies | 70 | 73 | 67 |
| Don't know | 1 | 1 | 1 |

| Q Is Britain less likely to be attacked because it has nuclear weapons? | all % | boys % | girls % |
|---|---|---|---|
| Less likely | 38 | 42 | 33 |
| More likely | 61 | 57 | 65 |
| Don't know | 1 | 1 | 2 |

● *Business Decisions Ltd conducted 422 interviews with teenagers between the ages of 15–18 in 20 locations around the country.*

Television Times, *10–16 December 1963*

## Nuclear Winter

There seems no doubt that a nuclear war would probably make the world totally uninhabitable. In November 1983 at a major international scientific conference held in Washington DC, a report stated that even a 'limited' nuclear war could initiate a climatic catastrophe which would kill many hundreds of millions of people who survived the immediate effects of the war, or who lived in areas remote from the conflict. There are several theories regarding what the world would be like climatically following nuclear war, but one which has wide support currently is that much of the globe would be too cold to sustain life.

## Arms Spending versus Alternatives

*PROPOSAL OF THE AEROSPACE SHOPS STEWARDS COMMITTEE, LUCAS INDUSTRIES*

This group put forward a plan for redeployment for peaceful purposes of existing resources, including manpower, used for military purposes. Though it proposed many useful things that would maintain, or even increase, employment, the plan was rejected by the management and ignored by successive British governments.

**The Brandt Report** (1980)   This was called 'North–South – a programme for survival'. It argued that huge sums spent on weapons and space
used up many resources which could otherwise help solve urgent world
problems. For example, the military use of oil equals half the oil consumed
by all the developing states except China.

**Use of valuable skills for war purposes**   About two-fifths of the
world's scientists and engineers are now involved in work related to military
research and development. Some eminent scientists, when they realised the
consequences and effects of nuclear weapons, refused to be involved further
in their development. For example, Robert Oppenheimer, who directed the
development of the US atomic bomb, refused to take part in further atomic
research work.

Distribution of world military expenditure 1971 and 1980

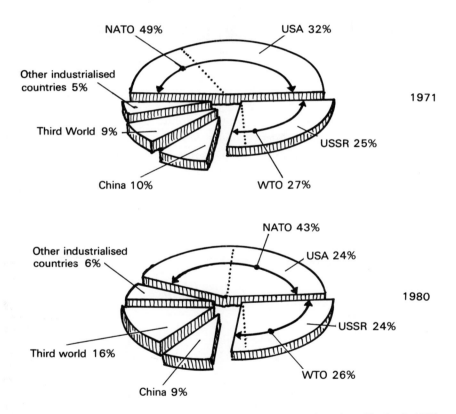

*Stockholm International Peace Research Institute Yearbook 1982*

**Arms spending versus higher living standards**   For many years
military spending has been justified partly on the grounds that it helps to
create jobs and to stimulate an economy. Increased wealth is created which
leads to greater demand for many consumer goods, thus helping businesses.

149

Military spending and economic growth

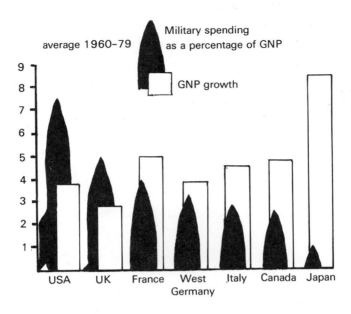

The economy has higher economic growth expressed in terms of the Gross National Product (broadly defined as the value of the goods and/or services produced in a year). Now some critics, including some eminent economists, have argued that military spending has adverse effects on an economy in terms of higher taxes and inflation, and retards the development of education, health services and housing.

The money required to provide adequate food, water, education, health and housing for everyone in the world has been estimated at $17 billion a year. It is a huge sum of money ... about as much as the world spends on arms every two weeks.

New Internationalist

*TGWU, Our Wider Aims, 1979*

## Alternatives to Nuclear War

Unilateralists argue that someone has to take the lead in disarming. The multilateralist argument that nuclear weapons must be retained as a bargaining weapon to force the other side to negotiate is false since so far arms negotiations have achieved little.

The Campaign for Nuclear Disarmament (CND) is the main pressure group or organisation seeking support for unilateralism in Britain. While it is not linked to any political party, and has supporters among all main political parties, its main strength comes from pacifists, conscientious objectors and left-wing opponents of nuclear weapons.

Many religious people, including some Christians, argue that the mere possession and threat to use nuclear weapons even in retaliation is immoral. The 'just war' conditions of discrimination (no killing of innocent civilians) and proportionality (not doing harm and damage out of all proportion to the ends to be gained) are difficult to satisfy given the power of nuclear weapons. It would be better to allow an invader to occupy Britain rather than to resort to nuclear weapons. This does not mean accepting the idea, 'better red than dead', as opponents tend to label this approach, since there are many ways, violent and non-violent, of continuing a struggle against an enemy rather than surrendering totally. Options are:

- forms of alternative defence suggested on page 154.
- total non-co-operation and passive disobedience.

---

The scale and the horror of modern warfare – whether nuclear or not – make it totally unacceptable as a means of settling differences between nations.

*Pope John Paul II, Coventry 1982*

---

It would be better to suffer a physical defeat than moral defeat.

*John Stott, Issues facing Christians Today, 1984*

War will be with us till that distant day when the conscientious objector receives the same prestige and respect in our society that the military hero does today.

*John F Kennedy*

# ACTIVITIES

1. Name the key Western strategy used to justify the arms race or multilateral disarmament. Do you agree with it?

2. In 1953 the US President, General Eisenhower, said: 'Every gun that is made, every warship launched, every rocket fired, signifies in the final sense a theft from those who hunger and are not fed, those who are cold and not clothed.' Find the extract(s) in this section which support this point of view. Do you agree with this viewpoint?

3. Suggest three ways a US–Soviet nuclear war might start even if neither side intended such a war.

4. Briefly list four reasons why unilateralists argue that deterrence policy does not bring security. If you disagree with any of the four, give reasons why.

5. If arms spending was greatly reduced in Britain, suggest other ways in which money could be spent which would immediately benefit the majority of the population.

6. Define the two following terms, making clear the difference between them: (a) proliferation (b) escalation.

7. What is you opinion on two of the questions asked by the Business Decisions Ltd on page 148? Explain why there is a contradiction in the thinking of the views expressed by the majority.

8. What do you think the cartoonist who drew 'Unemployed, Deployed' was trying to convey?

9. Comment briefly on the chart on military spending and economic growth on page 150. Note in particular comparisons between the USA and Japan.

10. Explain what is meant by:
    (a) 'better red than dead'  (b) 'moral defeat'.

11. Hold a class discussion on whether or not there is likely to be a nuclear war in the next 50 years. Alternatively, list six points for and against the chances of a nuclear war during the time mentioned.

# 9.3  Civil Defence Versus Social Defence

## Civil Defence Policy

### Definition of civil defence

Civil defence ... includes any measures not amounting to actual combat for affording defence against any form of hostile attack by a foreign power or for depriving any form of hostile attack by a foreign power of the whole or part of its effect.

*Civil Defence Act, 1948*

**Credible defence**  The National Council for Civil Defence (NCCD) wants the government to adopt a long-term civil defence strategy which allows for the provision of shelters for the whole population. Without them it argues that the public will have no faith in the government's civil defence policies.

**Government policy on civil defence**  Since the 1950s the British government's position has always been that it would not be able to protect the mass of the public in the event of a nuclear attack. The problem is partly the immense cost involved. A high quality domestic nuclear underground shelter protected with steel or concrete cost about £7000 in 1981. An effective national shelter campaign on the scale of that in Switzerland or Sweden cost about £10 billion in 1985. There is no guarantee that if large sums were spent on civil defence an attacker would not increase the scale of his attack to counter the effects of increased spending on defence.

In 1980, the government produced a booklet *Protect and Survive*, which contained details on how the ordinary family could build a makeshift refuge inside their home. This was later withdrawn after receiving heavy criticism for being totally inadequate, as the measures recommended would provide little real protection for most people in the event of a nuclear attack.

# Social Defence – An Alternative to Military Defence

In general the means of force or defence are highly concentrated in most countries within the ranks of the military and police forces. Despite the lack of participation of most of the civilian population in defence, except perhaps through voluntary militias and forms of civil defence or compulsory military service for the young, no government can survive without the passive support of its population.

Social defence represents a form of territorial defence recommended by pacifists and advocates of non-violent resistance. It is based on the idea that all the civilian population can effectively participate through means of decentralised network of alliances, and represents the non-violent equivalent of guerilla warfare.

The essence of social defence is the widespread non-co-operation in opposition to military aggression, foreign occupation, political repression or the suspension of human rights by means such as boycotts, strikes, demonstrations, sabotage (for example the destruction of information and records), and the creation of alternative (parallel) institutions for government, media, transport and education.

---

Protecting ourselves from our neighbours is the path of Arms and leads to war! Protecting our neighbours from ourselves is the path of disarmament, and leads to peace.

*Bernard Benson*, The Peace Book, *1981*

---

**Special nuclear bunkers** A number of shelters have been built to house political leaders and key personnel if a nuclear war seems close. This is justified on the grounds that it makes Britain's nuclear deterrent credible, since leaders would survive an initial attack and be able to wage a nuclear war.

*'But you haven't heard the best bit yet. After they bought me enough nuclear weapons to kill them all several times over. I asked for £300 million more for a bunker to enable me to do it in safety . . . and they gave it to me'*, The Pacifist, *July 1982*

Dai Owen, CND Publications

## Nuclear Free Zones (NFZs)

Some local authorities in Britain object to the government's policy of civil defence such as asking the public to build their own nuclear shelters and to co-operate with civil defence. They argue that if people believe a nuclear war can be survived then it becomes more likely. Only by realising that we could not survive such a war can we continue to avoid it. In June 1981, 70 local authorities, notably in Greater London, Wales and parts of the North, declared their areas 'nuclear free zones'. This involved some councils asking the government not to transport or dump nuclear waste in the area and not to site nuclear weapons or nuclear military installations there. Local council staff were instructed not to take part in civil defence planning.

**De-glorification of war and violence**   Evidence of violent events are all round us, whether we look at news reports from the radio or television, or see the videos and war magazines in bookshops and the wide range of war games which are readily available.

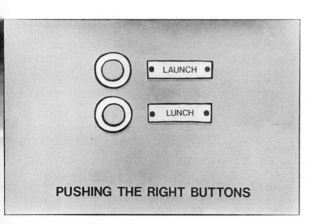

PUSHING THE RIGHT BUTTONS

Pushing the right buttons by Erica Rothenberg

Crown him the Lord of Peace
Whose will so long undone
Obeyed – shall make all war to cease
And man to be at one

*Hymn No 480*, Songs of Praise

Onward Christian soldiers
Marching as to war
With the Cross of Jesus
Going on before.

*S Baring-Gould, 1834–1924*

## THE HAPPY WARRIOR

His wild heart beats with painful sobs
his strain'd hands clench an ice-cold rifle
his aching jaws grip a hot parch'd tongue
his wide eyes search unconsciously.
He cannot shriek.
Bloody saliva
dribbles down his shapeless jacket.
I saw him stab
and stab again
a well-killed Boche.
This is the happy warrior,
this is he . . .

*Herbert Read, 'The Happy Warrior', Jon Silkin (Ed.),*
*The Penguin Book of First World War Poetry, 1979*

## ACTIVITIES

1. If the government provided nuclear shelters for all the population this would be an example of:
   **(a)** social defence   **(b)** credible defence   **(c)** civil defence   **(d)** alternative defence   **(e)** conventional defence.

2. Which one of the following declared itself a nuclear weapon free zone in March 1982?   **(a)** Wales   **(b)** England   **(c)** Scotland   **(d)** Northern Ireland.

3. Which word in the short extract from 'Onward Christian Soldiers' informs us that the writer is not referring to actual physical combat? What type of war or struggle did the writer of the hymn have in mind?

4. Write one sentence suggesting a connection between Erika Rothenberg's painting and war and peace issues.

5. Suggest some reasons (political, historical, economic, geographical) why Switzerland is in a better position to undertake a massive nuclear shelter programme than Britain.

6. In hymn 480, Songs of Praise, explain what is meant by   **(a)** 'will so long undone'   **(b)** 'man to be at one'.

7. Would you agree that the extract from 'The Happy Warrior' by Herbert Read deglorifies war? If so, explain in what way it does this. What part does irony play in the title or actual poem?

8. The ostrich cartoon comes from the CND's civil defence publication. Which one of the following does the cartoon best typify?

   (a) Precautions to take in the event of a nuclear explosion

   (b) Non-participation in government civil defence planning

   (c) Inadequacy of present government civil defence policies

   (d) A form of non-violent resistance according to the principles of social defence.

9. Suggest ways in which war and violence can be de-glorified.

10. Have a class discussion or debate on one of the following themes:

   (a) arguments for and against social defence as an alternative to other means of defence;

   (b) whether attempts should be made to de-glorify violence and war and, if so, how?

11.
> Gorbachev must secure peace abroad if his country is to advance at home. . . . Never before have the two issues – the development of the Soviet economy and world security – been so intimately connected. Now., as never before, the West must bear its share of responsibility for both.
>
> Christian Schmidt-Hauer, *Gorbachev — The Path to Power*, 1986

   (a) Explain what is meant by the comment that developments in the Soviet economy are linked to the issue of world security? (See pages 143, 149–50.)

   (b) Find out what Gorbachev has done since becoming Soviet leader to promote peace abroad and to introduce economic reforms at home.

   (c) What does the author mean by the comment that the West must bear part of the responsibility for both progress in the Soviet economy and improvements in world security?

# 10 PEACEKEEPING, PEACEMAKING AND SOLVING LARGE-SCALE CONFLICTS

## 10.1   Avoiding Conflicts and Maintaining Peace

### Preventing or Ending War

Items 1, 2 and 4 below are methods which have been used to prevent war, while 3 is a method which has been tried to end wars.

**1.   Balance of power**   It was on this principle that hope was placed for maintaining peace before the First World War. However, Europe became divided into two heavily armed camps and a relatively minor incident, the assassination of the Archduke Ferdinand of Austria at Sarajevo, was enough to start a major war.

**2.   Collective security**   The League of Nations from 1919 hoped to construct peace on this principle. If all the League members agreed to keep the peace, and to unite in opposition to any aggressive state, this would discourage any country from waging war. Unfortunately, this idea also failed since:

**(a)** all countries were too selfish to apply the principle;

**(b)** the largest countries were not members or only members for part of its life, for example the United States never joined and the USSR was not admitted until 1933.

The United Nations from 1945 was also based on collective security. However, it did include the largest states, the USA and the USSR, as members. In any case it could be argued that this principle was invalidated by:

**(a)** the Cold War divisions between East and West;

**(b)** the growth of nuclear weapons.

**3. Disarmament** If arms races could be stopped, and the means of waging war limited, this would prevent war. (For details of efforts made to secure disarmament see Chapter 9.)

**4. Boycott** Both the League of Nations and the United Nations have imposed boycotts at times (the prevention of arms or certain goods reaching a country) as a means of discouraging or stopping acts of aggression. However, for political reasons (self-interest generally) states have not always been willing to impose effective sanctions. An oil embargo of Italy in the 1930s, if fully carried out, would have prevented Mussolini's aggression against Ethiopia. A serious economic boycott of South Africa would have led to changes in apartheid far more rapidly. President Carter banned the export of grain to the USSR because of the latter's invasion of Afghanistan in 1979. However, President Reagan relaxed the ban because of the pressure from Mid-West farmers in the USA.

**5. Peacekeeping** See below.

**6. Arbitration** See page 166.

# Peacekeeping

**Definition and purpose** Peacekeeping takes place when a person or group helps

**(a)** to keep antagonists apart or separate,

**(b)** to maintain peace when a fight or dispute has ended and

**(c)** to prevent a renewal of a conflict.

An example at the small group level might be a prefect, teacher or parent intervening to stop children fighting or continuing a quarrel. At a larger level peacekeeping might involve an invitation to an international force to intervene between two opponents. In this case its role is one closer to policing than soldiering. Instead the hope is that it will be able to create peaceful and stable conditions which make it easier for the leaders of the warring sides to get together to solve their dispute, possibly helped by outside peacemakers.

**Types of peacekeeping** Sometimes UN peacekeeping forces have acted merely as a buffer presence, keeping two hostile groups and armies apart, as in the case of the UN forces which have operated on the Lebanon–Israeli border. Alternatively, the UN may operate within a state to help a government keep law and order, for example the Congo (Zaire), Cyprus and the Lebanon. A national force can perform a similar role, as undertaken by the British Army in Northern Ireland.

## Participation in peacekeeping

**1. United Nations operations** Under Article 43 of the UN Charter, member states are required to keep part of their armed forces for UN operations. Examples of these are the following:

- Middle East 1956–67 (guarding the Israeli–Egyptian frontier)
- Congo (Zaire) 1960–4
- Cyprus 1964–74
- The Lebanon 1978–

The general principles covering such interventions are that the forces should not include members of the Security Council or anyone whose political interests are involved. In addition the forces should not fire except in self-defence, nor take sides in a dispute.

The earliest peacekeeping operations after 1945 involved the presence of observers as in Greece (1947), Palestine (1948) and Indonesia (1948).

**2. Non-UN operations** Apart from operations under the flag of the UN, other peacekeeping activities have included:

- A Commonwealth force which ensured that the transfer to independence and majority rule took place with the minimum violence and disorder in Rhodesia, which on independence became Zimbabwe (1980).
- A predominantly African force (organised by the OAU) which tried to end the civil war in Chad.
- The multinational force, consisting of contingents from the United States, France, Italy and Britain, which went to Beirut in 1982.

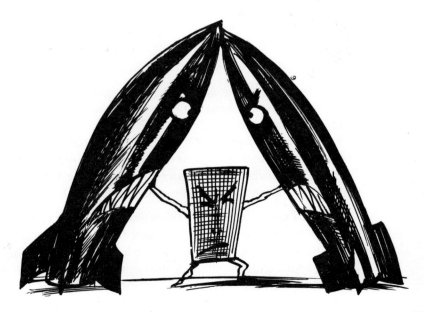

*United Nations Department of Public Information, September 1979*

# Strengths and Weaknesses of Peacekeeping

## Advantages

---

Is the deployment of a few thousand men really relevant to a world full of nuclear weapons?

Yes. Peacekeeping has become essential to the survival of the world, for two reasons.

**1.** The immediate future. This is a moment when big powers are in danger of colliding on equal terms in areas where there are no clear rules of conduct – something new in the last decade. Outside Europe, neither superpower is sure of the other's intentions. If things get out of control, both may be glad of a fire brigade at short notice.

**2.** In the longer term the development of peacekeeping is fundamental to world peace. The frustrations of disarmament efforts have caused people to view peacekeeping with new respect, and ask whether it is not at least as important. Clearly disarmament is desirable. But would people necessarily stop fighting if we reduced the level of arms, even down to bows and arrows?

The key to peace lies not only in the level of arms, but in the tools and techniques of preventing them from being used. Foremost among these is peacekeeping.

It has had its setbacks and humiliations. But it also has a formidable track record, in saving lives and helping to resolve conflict at little cost.

*Hugh Hanning,* United Nations Peacekeeping – 40 years on and the Way Ahead, *1985*

---

## Disadvantages

**1.** It may freeze rather than solve a conflict. Peacekeeping may result in a situation of 'negative peace' if no efforts are made at peacemaking. What this means is that relations between former antagonists may remain unfriendly, with both sides harbouring grudges and waiting for a chance to reopen hostilities, because of the continuation of some unresolved problem. Priority might be given by those making the peace terms to law and order considerations rather than to reforms (in the interests of greater freedom and justice) for groups seeking redress of their grievances or complaints.

One problem with the League Covenant (the rules governing the League of Nations) from 1919 was that peace tended to be interpreted as a situation of no change or of preserving the status quo or the existing territorial frontiers of the victors after the First World War. The League provided no effective means by which territorial changes could be brought about peacefully. As a result, discontented states such as Germany, Italy and Japan, eventually resorted to aggression.

**2.** UN peacekeeping has only been effective under certain limited conditions. For the most part, the UN has only stopped conflicts in cases where either the United States and the Soviet Union feared a major East-West nuclear confrontation and worked together to stop a conflict escalating, or in very local conflicts. In many conflicts the UN has not been closely involved. Examples are the present troubles in Iran and Iraq, Afghanistan, Kampuchea and El Salvador.

---
## ACTIVITIES
---

1. Name the type of methods represented by the examples below used for preventing or stopping conflict:

   (a) the system of opposing alliances in Europe before the First World War

   (b) stopping trade or any form of exchange with a particular country

   (c) working together in a common organisation to prevent war

   (d) division of India into two states, so that the Muslems could live in a new country, Pakistan (1948), apart from the Hindus.

2. (a) The Versailles Treaty is given in this chapter as an example of 'negative peace'. What grievances or complaints did the Germans have against this treaty?

   (b) What was meant by the appeasement policies of Britain and France towards Germany? Can you find any examples from history or from your own experience where appeasement has succeeded?

   (c) Do you think the Second World War might have been prevented if Britain and France had been willing to use force to stop Hitler in the mid-1930s, as in the case of the German reoccupation of the Rhineland (1936)?

---

## Peacemaking

**Peacemaking: a definition**   This involves measures to solve a conflict permanently to the satisfaction of the various groups or individuals involved. Sometimes individuals or groups are not willing to disclose their real grievances to outsiders, and it may take time before a peacemaker can find out the causes of the conflict and help the participants to settle their differences. If the peacemaker is effective, positive peace results. As in the case of a doctor, the peacemaker looks for the real cause of the sickness of a patient, so that he can treat and cure the 'patient' rather than merely giving 'pills' to cope with the symptoms.

**Peacemaking skills**   Usually those most successful in helping end disputes, at various levels from domestic to international conflicts, have relevant knowledge, experience or skills in handling others. These people could be known as mediators, negotiators, counsellors, intermediaries or facilitators. Note in particular the following:

**1. The ability to win the confidence and co-operation of others** If a peacemaker is able to reach an understanding with the people he is dealing with, he is likely to gain their friendship and respect. Many of the relevant attributes and qualities, such as open-mindedness, patience and tact, have been discussed in Chapter 7.

**2. Personal strength and self-confidence** A peacemaker has to have the determination and confidence to cope with stressful or tense situations, and the ability to encourage others through advice and suggestions to resolve their problems.

**3. Knowledge about conflict as a subject** Relevant subjects, including history, sociology, economics, politics, social psychology, peace or religious studies, help provide an insight into the causes of conflict at various levels and the possible remedies, as indicated particularly in Chapters 1, 3, 7 and 8. A peacemaker can help others, with opposing views, values or perceptions, to see a situation more realistically, so that they can approach problem-solving from a common viewpoint.

**Who is involved?** All of us may be involved occasionally in settling conflicts. Parents and teachers, youth and church or social workers, marriage guidance counsellors, industrial relations experts, politicians or diplomats may all act as peacemakers in their work.

**When peacemaking is particularly relevant** Many conflicts or disputes cannot be settled by applying rules or laws as might be done in a school, court of law or sports contest by a head teacher, judge or referee. Often there is no question of one side being absolutely right in a legal or moral sense and the other side being totally wrong. Rather the disputes involve how people react to and get on with each other. In these cases there are no clear rules or guidelines. Such disputes occur in marriages (husband and wife), industrial relations (management and workers) or clashes between groups in national and international crises, such as in Northern Ireland and the Middle East. These conflicts may be solved with the help of a mediator, negotiator or conciliator – all of whom may be called peacemakers.

**When peacemaking is necessary** If a fight takes place between two adults, or a war occurs between two major states, and in both situations the participants are roughly equal in strength and power, the two 'top dogs' involved often act as their own peacemakers solving their dispute themselves.

Peacemaking where a neutral outsider is involved is more likely to take place in the following situations:

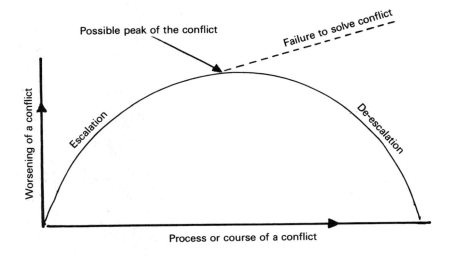

Possible peak of the conflict

Failure to solve conflict

Worsening of a conflict

Escalation

De-escalation

Process or course of a conflict

**1.** 'underdog' conflict, or a fight between two small states of roughly equal strength. The intervener may be a larger neighbouring state or the forces and diplomacy of an international organisation, such as the United Nations. This resembles the situation at the individual or small group level where a parent or teacher stops and possibly solves a conflict between two youngsters or pupils.

**2.** 'topdog–underdog' conflict, or war between two states unequal in strength. This situation resembles a conflict between a landlord and tenant, the government and an individual citizen, a parent and child, a big bully and a small person, or the rich and the poor. Naturally, it is not always the one presumed the stronger who wins (assuming no outside intervention) as the biblical story of David and Goliath shows.

**3.** 'topdog' conflict. An example is the Cold War between the USA and the USSR, the leaders of the rival blocs.

*détente is...* ...the exchange of sweet nothings.

*détente is...* ...covering up his treaty violations.

*détente is...* ...knowing when to give something for nothing.

*détente is...* ...starting a war in Angola.

*détente is...* ...thinking it can be stopped by détente.

*détente is...* ...getting fired for détente.

VAROOMSHKA

The Guardian, 5 January 1976

164

# Escalation and De-escalation of a Crisis

The process of escalation has been discussed in Chapter 1. Peacemaking may be particularly necessary at a critical point of a crisis, for example when a country is on the verge of war, or if a country is pondering whether to use nuclear weapons when a conventional war has reached a stalemate. Thus right decisions need to be made to prevent the situation getting worse. The 'Galtung Triangle' (see page 19) indicates how a crisis might be averted, or how a crisis situation can be gradually solved or de-escalated, through changes in attitudes, behaviour and the removal of any situation of injustice or lack of freedom. (See also Chapters 7, 8 and 12 for relevant ideas.)

# Peacemaking in Practice

Examples of ways conflicts have been ended are the following:

**1. Doing nothing about it** Sometimes a problem or conflict solves itself or gets forgotten since **(a)** another conflict may come up that is more important, **(b)** the participants may not think it so important after all, **(c)** a solution may emerge without anyone having to worry about it.

**2. Bargaining/trading** The mediator or peacemaker may help the participants reach a compromise of mutual benefit. Sometimes when there are many participants involved, swap deals can be arranged so that X loses something to Y, Y to Z and Z to X, so that all are content with the final result.

**3. Separation** The best solution might be for the warring groups to cut off links with each other so that they live separately, for example divorced couples or a country that becomes two. Many strong religious or cultural communities live apart in certain countries but co-operate where necessary. Examples of such 'pillarised societies' are the Netherlands, Belgium and Malaysia.

**4. Small steps** Sometimes if a problem is broken down into various parts, a mediator might help those in dispute to reach agreement in a piecemeal fashion or by stages.

---

### *MORAL IN THE TALE OF THE BOY AND THE DRAGON*

A dragon had appeared in a town and the problem was how to get rid of it. The mayor ignored the help of a small boy and enlisted first the aid of the army and then the aid of three wise men. When their suggestions of force and bribery failed, the boy took action himself and went up to the dragon. He whispered in the dragon's ear a polite request to go – and the dragon simply left.

---

Who does the peacemaking in major civil and international conflicts?

Mediation and peacemaking is usually undertaken by representatives of states or an international or regional body. Examples are the following:

**1.** The United Nations mediators have included Count Bernadotte in the Near East until he was shot in 1948, and Dag Hammarskjold, the UN Secretary-General, in the Congo (now Zaire) until his death in 1961.

**2.** Henry Kissinger, the US Secretary of State, in the Middle East.

**3.** The Organisation of African Unity (OAU) worked in conjunction with the All-African Conference of Churches (AACC) in trying to resolve the Sudan civil war. (Under Article 51 of the UN Charter regional organisations can settle disputes within their regions with UN support.)

Peacemaking efforts may also be undertaken unofficially by organisations or individuals working in a private capacity as in the case of the Quakers (members of the Society of Friends) who risked their lives to try and solve the Nigerian–Biafran conflict 1966–70.


## Arbitration

This can be considered a form of peacemaking. It occurs when a dispute is given to an impartial outsider who pronounces judgement. Some disputes are referred to the International Court of Justice at The Hague, founded in 1899, which has been closely linked with the League and the United Nations. A major weakness is that it has no power of enforcement.

In 1902 in a boundary dispute between Chile and Argentina, King Edward VII was invited to arbitrate. On a new line running through the high Andes a huge statue of Christ was placed with the inscription that these two states would never go to war again.


## The Start of Real Peacemaking as a Life-long Process

More or less total disarmament (whether of nuclear weapons only or including conventional weapons), as envisaged in the Clark–Sohn plan (see Chapter 12, page 202), would not necessarily solve world security. Note the following:

**1.** New weapons or alternative ways of harming or hurting others may be developed by people motivated by greed, envy or revenge.

**2.** The major powers might face rebellion or retaliation from states which considered they had been unjustly treated or exploited in the past.

*'Soon as the western powers disarm, and the eastern powers disarm, we move in on them'*

The rich live in terror of their fellow robbers, presumably, for if they feared the wrath of the poor, the investment of their military budgets in genuine aid would buy more security than the most powerful weaponry.

*Colin Morris, Unyoung, Uncoloured, Unpoor (SCM)*

**3.**   The abolition of war and destructive weapons might be regarded as an advanced stage of human development. In this stage, people can concentrate on the process of creating real or positive peace (which includes the structural, mental and environmental dimensions) as outlined in the diagram in Chapter 1, page 19, and in implementing further measures to insure a safe and just future (see the proposals in Section 12.2, Chapter 12).

167

# The Cuban Crisis: A Case Study

## Key events before, during and after

1. **April 1961:** Bay of Pigs episode. US-trained Cuban exiles returned to Cuba in an attempt to overthrow Castro's reformist government. This ended in disaster as Castro was forewarned by spies. Castro subsequently declared Cuba a socialist republic.

2. **August 1962:** Missile sites in Cuba. Castro agreed to allow the USSR to build missile sites on Cuba (just 100 miles from Florida) in exchange for more Soviet aid. Photo coverage by US reconnaissance planes found evidence of these sites on 29 August.

3. **October 1962:** Build-up to crisis. At first President Kennedy thought the missiles might be purely defensive, but on 14 October reconnaissance flights found evidence that MRBMs (medium-range ballistic missiles) were being installed.

4. **22–7 October:** Cuban crisis. President Kennedy imposed a naval blockade to prevent any offensive weapons reaching Cuba, on 22 October. On 24 October UN Secretary-General U Thant wrote to both the Soviet and American leaders asking them to refrain from any step likely to lead to war, requesting the USSR to suspend all arms shipments, and the USA to suspend all search of ships bound for Cuba. Both leaders agreed on 25 October, but tension continued as Soviet technicians on Cuba continued work on missile sites while a Soviet ship was on its way to Cuba. On 26 October Khrushchev wrote to Kennedy promising to dismantle the missile sites if the USA guaranteed not to invade Cuba. Kennedy agreed as long as the dismantling of the missile sites was done under UN supervision. Khrushchev agreed and was praised by Kennedy in a TV broadcast for his 'statesmanlike decisions'.

5. **27 October:** End of crisis. Khrushchev ordered the ship en route to Cuba to return to the USSR.

6. **10 June 1963:** President Kennedy announced the end of US atmospheric tests. His speech was immediately printed in *Pravda*, the Soviet newspaper, and the USSR did not jam the Voice of America radio broadcasts.

7. **11 June:** The USSR withdrew its previous objection to a Western proposal to send observers to war-stricken Yemen.

8. **14 June:** The United States withdrew its objection to the Hungarian delegation taking its place at the UN.

9. **15 June:** Khrushchev congratulated President Kennedy on his speech during a public broadcast and announced Soviet discontinuation of the production of strategic bombers.

**10. June:** 'Hot line' telephone. A direct link between Moscow and Washington was installed so that if another crisis occurred the two leaders of the superpowers could communicate at once, so as to avoid misunderstanding and the outbreak of war in error.

**11. July–August:** Nuclear test ban treaty. The USA and the USSR agreed to ban atmospheric atom bomb tests.

**12. October:** The US President lifted the embargo on grain to the USSR. Both countries agreed not to orbit nuclear weapons in space.

**13. November:** Assassination of President Kennedy.

**Observations on the Cuban crisis** The Cuban crisis was solved peacefully since both sides realised that if either of them made a false move a nuclear holocaust could follow. In addition each leader made considerable efforts to understand the other's position and point of view.

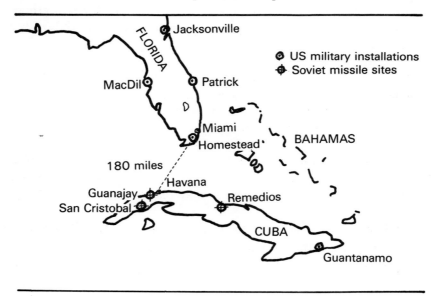

*The Cuban missile crisis, 1962*

Though Kennedy had taken a calculated risk, he allowed Khrushchev a 'face-saving' way out, the option of retreating from the predicament that the Soviet leader had created for himself. This can be contrasted with Austria's ultimatum to Serbia after the Sarajevo Murder (1914) which left Serbia with no real 'face-saving' alternative to saying no, thus putting into motion the events which led to the First World War.

Kennedy made no attempt to gloat over his victory and this marked the start of the period of détente.

The Cuban crisis remains a classic case of how to resolve a tense situation and to improve relations between bitter adversaries.

# ACTIVITIES

1. Find examples from your own experience, or from reference to the national or local press and history books of conflicts which were ended by one of the following means: (a) ignoring it (b) bargaining (c) separation (d) small steps, as listed on the previous pages.

2. In a group discuss under what circumstances the method recommended in 'Moral in the Tale' about the boy and the dragon might work in dealing with: (a) a stranger who is threatening you in a dark street (b) a territorial conflict between two countries.

3. Find out more details about UN peacekeeping operations in the Middle East and the Lebanon. Write a brief essay making out a case that the advantages of peacekeeping (based on the record since 1945) outweigh the disadvantages. Alternatively, or in addition, the class could divide into two groups, one side arguing a case that the UN peacekeeping operations have largely been a failure, the other side arguing that they have largely been a success.

4. An old Jewish custom relates to the burdening of a goat with the sins of a whole village and then driving the goat away. If humanity succeeded metaphorically in putting all the major weapons on the back of the goat and driving it out of the village, what problems might remain? How could these be resolved?

5. 'They will beat their swords into ploughshares and their spears into pruning hooks' (Isaiah 2:4). Explain the significance of this quotation. Who are the 'they'? When is this prediction to take place?

6. (a) How do the events during and immediately after the Cuban Crisis in 1962 show how good relations can be built up by a series of small steps?

   (b) Find examples of how East–West relations worsened after Kennedy's death.

7. Many talk about a solution to Ulster's problems, but few are prepared to say what the problem is. The reason is simple. The problem is that there is no solution.

   *Richard Rose*

   'Ireland Unfree shall never be at peace', Pro-IRA slogan in support of the 1981 hunger strike of Bobby Sands and others.

   Proposals for the future of Northern Ireland include the following:
   (a) independence; (b) separate states for both Northern Ireland and Eire under a central government; (c) federal Ireland with varying degrees of devolution for the North; (d) federal union of England, Wales, Scotland, Northern and Southern Ireland; (e) power-sharing in Northern Ireland, with final authority

resting with the British government;   (f) United Ireland under Dublin rule;
(g) direct rule of Ulster from London;   (h) Dublin and London share
responsibility for governing the North.

SUNDAY EXPRESS

OCTOBER 24, 1982

"The only solution to the Irish problem is to understand that no solution works"

London Express Service

Sunday Express, *24 October 1982*

Answer the following questions based on the above material:

(i) Suggest who is likely to be the main opponents of each of the above
proposals for the future of Northern Ireland.

(ii) Which one or two of the above do you think has the best chance of success?
Have you any other suggestions not mentioned above?

(iii) Who are the two people in the cartoon 'Solutions to the Irish Problem'?
What events during the period 1980–2 might have inspired this cartoon?

(iv) Explain briefly why it is difficult to determine what a 'free Ireland' means.

# 10.2   Role Playing and Simulation Exercises

## Role Playing

An actor in a play, film or TV serial performs a role, interpreting the character and life of someone else. In like manner, each of us may undertake different duties and responsibilities during a week. For example a young person might perform the roles of an elder brother, pupil or part-time assistant in a shop.

**Role conflict**   Sometimes a person experiences stress if his or her roles or duties conflict. An employee might be torn between loyalty to a trade union which has called a strike and loyalty to firm and family, if he or she is in need of money and his wife or her husband does not support the strike.

A person might experience stress when another person sees him or her in a role other than that they normally perform. For example, women may experience sexual harassment at work when males see them as sex symbols rather than as work colleagues. Girls at school may get frustrated if the school authorities expect them to follow certain subjects such as cookery, needlework or childcare studies or art, when they would prefer to study science or foreign languages.

**Who am I?**   Often we do not appear to be the same person to others since we may behave differently according to our roles and the different people we encounter. Some people have difficulty in finding out who they really are and discovering their real individual identities. Often a person acts according to the expectations of others since his role might be fairly closely defined, either occupationally or legally, as in the case of lawyers or doctors.

## ═══════════ ACTIVITIES ═══════════

1.  Explain how the extract on 'role playing' refers to women's rights? List the main roles that you have to play yourself in the course of an ordinary week.

2.  Borrow a book of fiction and summarise briefly how two of its characters play a number of roles in the course of the story. If possible find a copy of *The Admirable Crichton* by J M Barrie, which explains how the butler and the owner of a large house change roles when they are marooned, together with members of the owner's family, on a deserted island.

3.  ## Iran–Iraq simulation

Following a long period of disputes between Iran and Iraq, Iraq declared war on Iran in September 1980, aiming to bring about the downfall of the Khomeini regime.

Assume that you are an expert peacemaker, with experience in settling disputes and working out solutions acceptable to warring parties to a conflict after a period of negotiations. You have been asked by the UN Secretary General to visit the area with a team of four advisers to meet two representatives each from Iran and Iraq to discuss measures which might lead to a ceasefire and on to an end of the war.

**Background**   The peacemaking group of five is expected to become acquainted with recent developments affecting Iran, Iraq and the surrounding areas since 1970.

The two representatives of Iran and Iraq should be familiar with the point of view and relevant current policies concerning the dispute of their respective governments.

**Activity**   The UN group should hold a meeting first chaired by the expert peacemaker, to be followed by another with the four representatives from Iran and Iraq. However, participants may wish to vary the number of meetings, the number of participants, or the procedure.

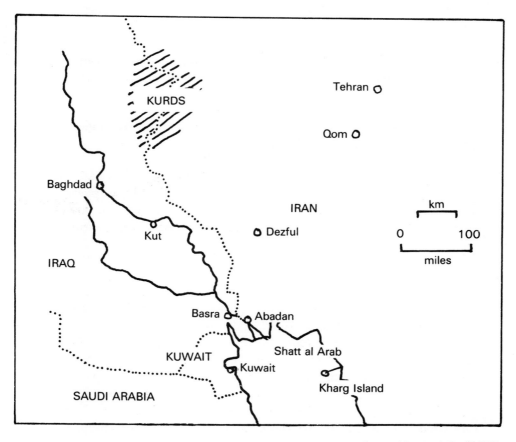

*Iran and Iraq and the Gulf War*

4. **Decision-making exercise**

This activity could first be undertaken as an individual project and then followed by a group discussion to assess the options which were chosen.

If you were a candidate in an election to become the American President, which of the following positions would you take on nuclear issues? Give reasons. Would you keep to that platform after you had been elected?

(a) A nuclear freeze (a situation in which the development and testing of all nuclear weapons and delivery systems would cease on both sides) should take place between the USSR and the USA. The problem of verification would remain.

(b) The US weapons system in Europe should be unilaterally dismantled as a peaceful move. The hoped for denuclearisation of East and West Europe would result in worldwide arms control talks between the United States and the Soviet Union.

(c) The USA should seek agreement with the USSR for cuts in the number of nuclear weapons and adjustments in the types of weapons so real equality is achieved in nuclear forces.

(d) The USA should halt all funding for new weapons to demonstrate good faith and relay a peace message to the USSR. If the Russians respond in like manner, gradual disarmament can begin.

(e) The USA must become a strong military power, both in conventional and nuclear arms, and must spend what is necessary.

(f) The USA should develop a strategic defence system (popularly known as 'Star Wars'), that can destroy enemy nuclear missiles before they explode on the USA or in Western Europe. This will discourage the Russians from threatening a nuclear attack and lead to eventual reduction of East–West nuclear arsenals.

5. **Group exercise**

**Background**   Country 'A' is large and powerful, taking a leading role in the arms race. For ten years the scientists have been working on a new weapon (code name Violet), a missile (range 7000 km) with a high degree of accuracy on target. The weapon can be launched from land, submarine or aircraft and cannot be detected by radar or satellite. However, the country has just signed a UN treaty banning further production of a certain category of weapons, to which this one belongs. Country 'A' is experiencing economic difficulties – inflation, unemployment and a rising level of imported goods. The Prime Minister is not sure what to do and so invites representatives from various groups to an informal meeting to discuss the problem. (Add other groups to this list if necessary.)

**Activity** One person should act the role of the Prime Minister, and one should act as Secretary, making notes of the main points made. One or two people could represent each concerned group (one represents the outside consultant). Allow time for preparing information to support the various positions taken by each group, or for including additional arguments. (Use this book and details from library sources in doing this.) The meeting should last about 45 minutes. The Prime Minister should prepare questions to ask each invited group.

What the groups want

The Army wants the country to remain a strong military power and to keep ahead in the arms race.

The scientists want their project to be fulfilled, having worked hard on it so far. They also want more funds for more weapons research in the future. This project will help as a precedent.

The Defence Department needs an increased defence budget since the rate of obsolescence of all weapons systems is high. They argue that money can be earned by selling some of the military know-how to our allies, particularly in developing countries. National security should be the first priority.

The industrial workers say that most defence work takes place away from large urban areas. If their factory closes, practically all the workforce of 12000 will lose their jobs and there are no other available jobs in the area.

The Trade Department believes that the government should allow more funds to create jobs. At present, for every billion dollars spent, only 76000 jobs can be developed in military programmes, as opposed to 100000 in civilian work. Scientists and engineers would contribute more to national welfare if employed in making technical advances in the manufacturing sector rather than in defence work. Nevertheless, the arms trade is profitable, particularly through exports to the Middle East. However, the department wonders whether we should continue to sell to this area, since it is thought to be one of the likely ways in which a world war might start.

The Social Security Department maintains that funds are urgently needed for more hospitals, schools and miscellaneous services for the old, unemployed and others, and for urban renewal. This is only possible if the government either increases taxes or cuts defence spending.

The Diplomats claim that to violate the treaty will weaken the UN and our efforts to get further disarmament and arms control measures accepted. As the new weapon cannot be detected by the usual methods, this will create more mistrust and lead to a further boost to the arms race, especially as the other side will try to get the new weapon for themselves.

The outside consultant says that there is a growing vigorous peace movement and many people, supported by a number of churchmen and famous scientists and doctors, want to freeze all production of new weapons. If this influence continues to increase, it could have an important impact on the next election.

### 6. Anglo-Soviet disarmament negotiations

The USA and the USSR agreed in a recent summit meeting to send three representatives each (consisting on the US side of the Secretary of State and on the Russian side the Minister for Foreign Affairs plus their advisors) to a conference to obtain substantial progress on disarmament, with the aim of signing *a wide-ranging test ban treaty*.

If necessary during the negotiations the representatives may return to their own country to consult the respective leaders or one or more special groups interested in the discussions. Once a treaty draft has been approved by the representatives of both sides, they must then get the approval of these special groups. A majority vote of these groups on each side (each group having one vote) guarantees approval of the draft. If both sides render a majority verdict then the negotiations will have succeeded. There are six groups on each side. Only in the event of a tie can the leader (the US and Soviet Heads of State) give the casting vote.

The special groups are as follows:

(a) On the US side: Joint Chiefs of Staff, State Department, Atomic Energy Commission, NATO allies, Congress, Consortium of American Peace Groups.

(b) On the Russian side: Joint Chiefs of Staff, Foreign Office, Soviet group of atomic scientists, Warsaw Pact allies, Supreme Soviet, Collective of Soviet Human Rights campaigners.

Each special group is represented by two people. They can be consulted by the negotiating team any time before a treaty draft stage is reached, and afterwards.

**The phases**   Pre-negotiating phase. Each team should decide first its aims and what type of proposals, compromises or conditions might be made.

Negotiating phase. The two teams meet to bargain and negotiate.

Post-negotiation. Each side has to convince its own special groups of the worth of any draft treaty agreed.

In total 16 persons are involved on each side. If your whole group is less than 32 adapt the game accordingly, by having only one person representing each special group, and the negotiating teams to consist of only one advisor each supporting the respective foreign affairs specialists.

The broad details of any possible treaty would need to be established in written form. The pros and cons of including any of the following options (or others) in the treaty should be considered:

(i) forbids testing of nuclear weapons in atmosphere, water and underground

(ii) is linked to non-aggression treaty between US and USSR

(iii) is linked to non-aggression treaty between NATO (all US allies in Europe) and Warsaw Pact (all USSR allies in Europe)

(iv) leads to a reduction of nuclear arms by 50 per cent, and non-aggression pact between NATO and Warsaw Pact

or

(v) putting all nuclear resources and weapons under UN control.

7. (a) **Telephone Game**   Select a person to devise a short message of about 12 words. Then pass on the message by means of whispering from one person to the next. The last person in the chain says out aloud what he or she thinks the message is. This can be compared with the original. A discussion could follow on how failures in communication can contribute to conflict.

(b) **Rumour Clinic**   Six volunteers leave the room. One returns and is shown a picture or told a short story. He or she then describes it to the second volunteer who comes in. Then the second volunteer asks the third volunteer to come in and repeats the same information. Eventually the sixth volunteer repeats what he or she has just been told to the whole group. The group could then discuss the reasons for any discrepancy between the original and final versions.

# 11 HUMAN RIGHTS AND EAST–WEST CONFLICT

## 11.1 Human Rights and Responsibilities

Rights, both for individuals and states, are what people are likely to fight for, because they are necessary for a decent life. This section deals with the topic in more detail and relates it to the East–West conflict concerning human rights, an extreme form of the conflict over human rights between the right and the left in most democratic states.

A United Nations handbook for teachers on *Teaching Human Rights* (Second edition 1963) starts with this extract from Mrs Franklin D Roosevelt, 27 March 1958:

---

Where, after all, do universal human rights begin? In small places, close to home. . . . The neighbourhood he lives in; the school or college he attends; the factory, farm or office where he works. Such are the places where every man, woman and child seeks equal justice, equal opportunity, equal dignity without discrimination. Unless these rights have meaning there, they have little meaning anywhere.

---

The basic human needs of . . .
Food, clothing, shelter
should be the birthright of every human being.
But . . .
It is a duty to strive to earn a living, and learn a trade or skill.

Everyone has the right to work.
But . . .
The economic resources of the world must be organised, its sources of raw materials tapped and fully utilised, and the distribution of its products equitably regulated to make this possible.

Everyone has the right to education.

But . . .

It is the duty of parents and the authorities to ensure that every child is instructed in knowledge.

Every individual has the right to freedom of speech and self-expression, freedom of assembly, freedom of the press . . .

But . . .

It is the duty of each individual to respect the views of one another and abandon all forms of prejudice.

"All prejudices, whether of religion, race, politics, or nation, must be renounced, for these prejudices have caused the world's sickness. Every ruinous war with its terrible bloodshed and misery has been caused by one or other of these prejudices." (Bahá'í writings)

Every human being has the right to security of life and personal property.

But . . .

That right can only be possible in a world of peace and equality of personal status.

Everyone has the right to be governed justly with equal rights before the law.

But . . .

Man must be courageous enough to reject inhuman behaviour, rule by terror, death squads, slavery, and the 'non-person' syndrome – all such obscene acts which abuse the human rights of others.

No-one should live in fear; none should live in want.

*Extract from 'Universality, Human Rights, Peace', National Spiritual Assembly of the Bahá'ís of the United Kingdom*

---

# Rights and Responsibilities

The right to be cared for when ill has to be balanced by the responsibility to care for others.

The right to one's own possessions has to be balanced by the responsibility to respect what belongs to someone else.

The right to old age pensions and welfare benefits has to be balanced by the responsibility to pay taxes.

The right to walk out of doors unmolested has to be balanced by the responsibility not to harm others.

---

Rights also imply corresponding duties. Whatever is my right as a man is also the right of another.

*Thomas Paine,* Rights of Man

---

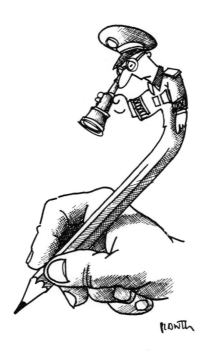

*Plantu*, La démocratie? Parlons-en!

## Individual versus Group Rights

**1.** Voting

The Western democratic ideal stresses that everyone should have the vote and that there should be equality of rights. However, there is the problem that one particular group may always be in a permanent majority, and laws may be passed which are considered unjust by the minority. The need arises, therefore, to protect the rights of minorities. This can be done by making laws protecting such rights.

Another solution is a form of power-sharing, though this tends to work best when no one group is numerically much greater than the others, as in Switzerland, the Netherlands or Malaysia.

**2.** Employment and education

To allow members of certain minority groups special rights infringes the principle of equality of rights. However, in the interests of good relations between different sections of a population a government might encourage giving deprived groups special advantages in such areas as access to higher education or certain jobs. This is called 'positive discrimination'.

**3.** The right to peace and quiet versus the right to make a noise

To some extent this is reflected in the clash between Article 12 of the Universal Declaration on Human Rights (the right to privacy) and Article 19 (the right to freedom of opinion and expression).

**4.** The right to work versus the right to strike.

# Left-wing versus Right-wing View of Human Rights

**Right-wing** or conservative elements tend to put stress on:

- Individual rather than collective rights, and the liberty of the individual.
- Civil and political rights associated with a democratic and free society, such as the right to vote, freedom of speech and worship.
- Private ownership of businesses (called private enterprise or capitalism).
- The right to own and bequeath property. This is recognised by Article 17 of the UN Declaration on Human Rights (1948).
- The limits of government intervention in the affairs of its citizens. This should be kept to a minimum to prevent clashes with the other rights above.
- The freedom to belong or not to belong to organisations such as trades unions.

**Left-wing** or socialist elements argue that:

- certain economic or social rights are necessary to remove the gaps between the rich and poor, the powerful and the powerless, without which political and civil rights are valueless. Some demand the right to work. This approach is reflected in Article 25 of the UN Declaration on Human Rights. Part I states:
  Everyone has the right to a standard of living adequate for the health and well-being of himself and of his family, including food, clothing, housing and medical care and necessary social services, and the right to security in the event of unemployment, sickness, disability, widowhood, old age or other lack of livelihood in circumstances beyond his control.
- a considerable degree of government intervention may be necessary in an economy and society to insure that these economic and social rights can be implemented.

# Inequality

Power in most states resembles a pyramid. A small group at the top tends to have most of the wealth, and together with the 'middle class' has most of the influence in political, economic and social matters. However, in a democracy all adults have the vote and need to be vigilant so as to protect their rights. Governments in such countries try to reduce inequalities of income and wealth and improve opportunities for people to better their conditions.

**Equality does not always mean justice**  Certain types of equality could be unjust, such as paying people the same wage despite the fact that their work varied in responsibilities or the amount of danger involved. Inequality does not necessarily mean injustice. Many roles in life, such as parent and child, senior civil servant and ordinary citizen, illustrate inequalities of power. However, although this power can be abused, it is not necessarily exercised to the disadvantage of the weaker.

---

It is startling to compare the life cycles of persons born into the higher socio-economic groups with those born into the lower. They have a four times better chance of surviving the first month of life. They are seven times less likely to leave school early. Consequently they are much more likely to go on to university and get a degree which makes them more than 20 times as likely as someone with GCE or similar qualifications to earn a salary that places them among the 10% of the population who possess about 90% of the wealth of the country.

*Adam Curle*, True Justice, *1981*

---

As *The Times* noted in an editorial called 'The Fashionable Conscience' in 1970, the Russian invasion of Czechoslovakia in 1968 and the complete suppression of any signs of independence or freedom did not cause anything like the indignation and numerous protests that erupted in the West over South African cricket. Neither was there much concern about the right-wing government in Brazil, which had been treating its own native Amerindian population and dissidents in a way far worse than anything that has occurred in South Africa.

"He that is without sin among you, let him first cast a stone . . ." — St. John, Chapter 8

*Dr Verwoerd, Prime Minister of South Africa, faces world criticism after the events at Sharpeville in 1960,* Daily Express, *28 March 1960*

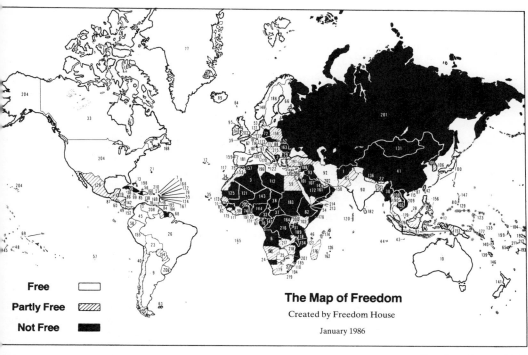

**The Map of Freedom**

Created by Freedom House

January 1986

Free ▭

Partly Free ▨

Not Free ■

*Freedom House, 1986*

# Free and Unfree Countries

**Military rule**   Military rule tends to be linked to a greater extent with forms of repression than civilian governments, with right-wing military regimes having a particularly bad record. Repression includes political detention, torture, executions and disappearances.

Studies have found that relating to the factors affecting military overthrows or coups d'états in Latin America, Asia and Africa:

- the higher the spending for military purposes, the greater the political instability;
- the greater the political instability, the greater the funds spent on the armed forces;
- the larger the sums put for military use, the lower is the growth rate of the economy.

**Prisoners of conscience and Amnesty International**   In over 50 per cent of the world's countries people are in prison for activities taken for granted in democratic countries, such as joining trades unions or political parties, publishing opinions or making speeches. For example, Dr Anatoly Koryagin was imprisoned in 1981 for condemning in the British medical journal *The Lancet* the misuse for political purposes of psychiatric treatment in the USSR.

Amnesty International is the best known organisation helping to release prisoners of conscience. No prisoner is supported who has used violence. One important method used by Amnesty is the sending of letters to the authorities of the relevant countries reminding the violators of human rights that the outside world is watching them. Sometimes the efforts of Amnesty get sentences reduced, prison conditions improved or the prisoners released.

## ACTIVITIES

1. Which of the following are rights and which are responsibilities or duties?

   (a) Respect the wishes of others for quiet and peace.

   (b) Need to study and learn.

   (c) Caring for others less fortunate than ourselves.

   (d) Opportunity for work and leisure.

   (e) Refusal to harass or molest strangers in the street.

2. Identify the sentence in the extract from 'Universality, Human Rights, Peace' (pages 178–9) which refers to civil and political rights.

3. What do you think the cartoon by Plantu (page 180) is saying? Name a country or countries where this cartoon would apply.

4. Obtain a copy of the United Nations Declaration of Human Rights. In what way do certain rights conflict with other rights?

5. Which article(s) of the UN Declaration of Human Rights refer(s) to basic human needs?

6. Article 13 of the UN Declaration states that everyone has the right to freedom of movement and residence within the borders of each state. How and why is this right restricted in the USSR and South Africa.

7. Illustrate from the history of Northern Ireland (between 1921–69) and from recent events in Sri Lanka how democracy can be a form of tyranny for a group if it is permanently in a minority for reasons of race, ethnicity or religion.

8. Based on the cartoon on page 182:

   (a) Provide full details about the Sharpeville incident, including causes and results.

   (b) Say what message you think the cartoonist is trying to convey. Is it linked with some of the press extracts above?

   (c) Name the leaders holding stones. Explain the labels on each of them. How is the cartoon relevant to the Old Testament story about the mote in your own eye?

**(d)** Find the misquote in the biblical quotation.

**(e)** For what reasons, and in what countries in the past, has stoning to death been the penalty. Is it still practised today in some countries?

9. Give examples of what is meant by the 'non-person' syndrome referred to in the extract from 'Universality, Human Rights, Peace'.

10. Look at the map of 'Free', 'Partly Free' and 'Not Free' countries on page 183. In small groups draw up about six to ten points or principles which might act as guidelines in deciding how to classify countries or societies into these three categories.

11. Answer the following questions on the items below.

**(a)** What contributions did they make to the promotion of human rights or basic freedoms?

**(b)** What form of oppression did each of them reduce or overthrow?

**(c)** Did any of them lead to war and perhaps to a new form of oppression?

**(i)** Magna Carta, 1215   **(ii)** Bill of Rights, 1689   **(iii)** American Declaration of Independence, 1776   **(iv)** French Revolution, 1789   **(v)** Revolts in Latin America, 1820s   **(vi)** Russian Revolutions, 1905, 1917   **(vii)** Independence of the Belgian Congo (now Zaire), 1960.

# 11.2   Human Rights, Ideology and the Cold War

Often bitter conflicts are difficult to resolve since participants are unable to appreciate how their opponents view a particular problem. An illustration of this is provided by the Cold War and the conflict between East and West over ideological matters and issues of human rights.

In this section are examples of various points of view. The first extract by Brian Crozier is an example of the hard right-wing point of view which sees little good in any aspect of communism or its ideology.

### NEVER TRUST COMMUNISTS OR THEIR BELIEF IN PEACE

Many people make the mistake of assuming that the Soviets are like ourselves, at heart decent human beings who long for peace, and with whom, given patience, one can surely reach an understanding . . . 'Surely,' some people think, 'their desire for peace must be genuine.' This is an easy, honest mistake to make. Unfortunately it is very dangerous. It is a state organised expressly for total repression at home and indefinite expansion abroad.

185

The Soviet Constitution of 1977 commits the Soviet Union to Marxism–Leninism, which may be summarised as follows: It is a law of history that capitalism inevitably evolves, via 'socialism', towards a communist ideal state that will ultimately comprise the whole of mankind. Only then can there be 'peace'. (Putting a Communist Party in power brings 'socialism', and is thus 'working for peace'.)

*Brian Crozier,* The Price of Peace, *1983*

---

# The Cold War and East–West Relations: Images of Ourselves and of the Other Side

Both the West and the Soviet bloc see themselves as defending the best of ideals. Each side tends to ignore its own defects or shortcomings, while stressing the drawbacks and ignoring the good points of the other side. Below is a chart summarising some of the characteristics, strengths and weaknesses of both the superpowers.

## The United States

**As seen by its supporters**   The United States is the chief democracy and champion of human rights in the world. It is a pluralistic system with freedom of the individual to join any political party or follow any religious belief. The United States is the leading capitalist country and supporter of private enterprise and the market economy.

It is an open society, for example the activities of political leaders can be discussed freely by the press; each individual is free to move within or to leave or enter the country. Tyranny and oppression is avoided since rulers and important officials can be replaced through free regular elections.

**As seen by its critics**   The weak are exploited by the strong. Money is 'king' and determines real power and influence, whether in politics, business or the law.

Goods and services are produced mainly for those who can afford to pay for them and not for those most in need. There is much poverty, unemployment and crime, and the welfare system is minimal.

Privacy is abused by the highlighting of scandal-type or sensational stories in the press. Minimum freedom exists for left-wing campaigners who wish to modify the system.

# The Soviet Union

**As seen by its supporters**  It is a 'true' democracy since the one-party communist system exists to serve the interests of the people, especially the majority who are ordinary workers, and the poor. There is special focus on economic and social rights, and the provision of adequate health and educational services for all, as well as the right to employment.

The government supports sport and culture, which helps enrich people's lives. Crime rates are low.

Eventually the state will become less important as the ultimate communist ideal society is arrived at, when people are primarily motivated by ideals of caring and self-sacrifice.

**As seen by its critics**  The country is highly élitist, that is to say it is ruled by members of the Communist Party (some 8 per cent of the people) who have most of the privileges.

The system restricts personal liberties and freedoms, and is like one giant organisation run for the benefit of the élite or party faithful. It is a closed system which means it is difficult to obtain news of events taking place in Russia and abroad.

The government discourages religious worship. Private enterprise is severely limited, and the country suffers from extreme standardisation and the lack of individual incentives.

# The Cold War

The following is a summary of recent developments relevant to the deterioration in East–West relations.

After the Helsinki Agreement, 1975, an increase in basic freedoms in the Soviet bloc would have been a sign for the US leader, President Carter, that Soviet leaders wanted to strengthen détente. This did not happen though the Russians did allow some Soviet Jews to emigrate. Instead Anatoly Shcharnansky, a champion of human rights, was imprisoned in February 1977. Many dissidents continued to be harassed, including Czech citizens who signed Charter 77 calling for human rights as promised at Helsinki.

In June 1979 President Carter and Leonid Brezhnev met to sign Salt II. In July the US Senate, angry over a supposed Soviet combat brigade in Cuba, refused to ratify this agreement. In December 1979, Soviet military intervention took place in Afghanistan. In retaliation the USA refused to participate in the Moscow Olympic Games. President Reagan took a hostile anti-Soviet stance and increased arms spending.

East–West relations deteriorated in 1981. From August 1980 a trade union movement, known as Solidarity and led by Lech Walesa, gained popularity in Poland and obtained some concessions from the government. In 1981 the

Russians, fearing that the Communist Party was losing its grip in Poland, intervened and Marshal Jaruzelski became leader and dissolved Solidarity. From November President Reagan gave increased US support to the opponents of the left-wing Sandinista government in Nicaragua and also to the right-wing government in El Salvador in its suppression of the revolt of many Salvadorans.

In March 1983 President Reagan announced the Strategic Defence Initiative (Star Wars) and in 1984 the Russians moved missiles into Eastern Europe in response to American deployment of new weapons (including Cruise missiles) into Western Europe. In November 1985 a Summit Conference in Switzerland gave the two leaders, Reagan and Gorbachev, an opportunity to appreciate the points of view of the other side.

## ──────── ACTIVITIES ────────

1. Find out more details about the items underlined in the section called 'The Cold War' and explain how they contributed to a worsening in East–West relations, following a period of relative thaw from 1963 until the late 1970s.

2. Bring the events underlined in the section called 'The Cold War' up to date by mentioning recent major developments in the Cold War.

---

*RELEASE OF SOVIET HUMAN RIGHTS CAMPAIGNER*

Mr Anatoly Shcharnansky was released from a Moscow prison in February 1986 after nine years in a Moscow prison. He had been imprisoned for being a spokesman for human rights. According to *The Times*, 14 February, he had not actually been tortured, but had suffered from hunger and cold and the deprivation of all mail in 1982. That year he decided he would have to stage a hunger strike. "I had to face up to the fact that I would probably have to starve myself to death in order to prove that I was alive."

---

**Five points against the West's record on human rights from the Russian viewpoint:**

1. The persecution of trade unions and the fierce suppression of strikes as has happened under Mrs Thatcher, notably in connection with the miners' strike.

2. The suppression of dissidents, members of progressive organisations and anti-war movements, for example actions against the women of Greenham Common.

3. Racial discrimination which affects tens of millions of blacks, Hispanics and Indians in America and immigrant workers in Western Europe.

**4.** The United States' support of undemocratic regimes. It finances and arms Pinochet's executioners, the death squads in El Salvador, South African racists and Israel which is still denying Arabs rights to their lands.

**5.** Britain's handling of the problems of Northern Ireland, for example its interrogation techniques and conditions inside the Maze prison.

**A view of Russia from the West:** As recently as four years ago, any Western journalist in Moscow could have contrasted such an attack in *Pravda* against a description of the silent groups who trudged around the snow of Pushkin Square each Human Rights Day, making their own grimly muted comment on 'Rights' in the USSR. Jewish people, Baptists, Catholics, would-be emigrants and dissidents would gather and occasionally one would pull a small banner from beneath a coat before being hustled away.

Such events would not be reported in Soviet press, and in any case such demonstrations have now ceased.

The West has been shocked by reports of methods used by the Soviet government to discourage opposition to its policies such as the use of psychiatric hospitals where opponents are deemed to have recovered when they again support the system wholeheartedly; exile and prison camps. However, intelligent Russians point out that there is a vast difference between such measures and those used during the total ruthlessness of Stalin's day.

―――――――――――――― **ACTIVITIES** ――――――――――――――

Find out more about the following:
**(a)** President Pinochet of Chile **(b)** the Maze Prison **(c)** Russian activities in Afghanistan **(d)** death squads in El Salvador **(e)** Alexander Solzhenitsyn and his book *One Day in the Life of Ivan Denisovitch* **(f)** Andrei Sakharov, a famous nuclear physicist and 'father' of Russia's hydrogen bomb **(g)** the women of Greenham Common.

## The United States and its Defence of Human Rights as seen by its Critics

The United States sees itself as the leading champion of freedom, democracy and human rights in the world. Blacks and other non-whites in this country point to the slowness with which the Federal government took action after 1945 to remedy the barriers which prevented them from enjoying full rights as citizens. Note, for example, the efforts of people like Martin Luther King, who campaigned peacefully for changes. Despite changes in the law, intolerance and racism have persisted. (See the article on the Ku Klux Klan, Chapter 3.) Many also criticise the United States for its 'neo-colonialism' and support of undemocratic oppressive governments.

**US support for undemocratic states**   The US image as the champion of human rights is spoilt for many people in the Third World by its military and economic support and aid for undemocratic repressive governments if they are right wing and anti-communist. Examples have been the Philippines under Ferdinand Marcos, South Korea and Batista in Cuba until he was replaced by the Marxist, Fidel Castro, in 1959.

Often the US government ignored the fact that when these right-wing governments were replaced by left-wing leaders, the latter did much more to help ordinary people and implemented much needed social reforms, for example as carried out by Castro in Cuba or the Sandinistas in Nicaragua from 1979 after the downfall of the US-backed Somoza dynasty, which had exerted one of the worst tyrannies in Latin America since 1934.

When the US withdrew support for these countries following their shift towards left-wing politics this tended to increase their reliance on the USSR and the communist bloc as occurred in Cuba from 1960 and Nicaragua from 1981.

Daily Telegraph, *14 July 1978*

**What a Western critic might say about Soviet democracy** Your system is not democratic according to our standards since (a) only one political party is permitted, the Communist Party (b) only one official candidate is offered at elections (c) the system of voting is such that observers know whether or not a voter has supported the recommended candidate. Only a system which has two or more political parties can be democratic, since it offers the electorate a choice between different candidates.

A Russian might reply that efforts are made to choose the best candidate when many are put forward at pre-election meetings.

---

*POLISH JOKE*

First Speaker: Do you know why a two party system would not work in Poland?
Second Speaker: No
First Speaker: Because the second party would become so popular that we would eventually return to a one party system.

---

## ACTIVITIES

1. Which one of the following countries has a common frontier with one of the two superpowers: **(a)** Hungary **(b)** El Salvador **(c)** Afghanistan **(d)** Nicaragua **(e)** Cuba?

2. Mention at least two articles of the United Nations Declaration on Human Rights (or parts of different articles) which you think the USSR attaches more importance to than the USA. Compare your results with your neighbour.

3. Crozier refers to the 'communist ideal state' in his extract (on pages 185–6). Identify the sentence in the chart about the two superpowers which describes briefly what this will be like.

4. Refer to the Garland cartoon from the *Daily Telegraph* (on page 190). What is a Russian dissident? How does the cartoon illustrate one important difference between the USA and the USSR?

5. Name three barriers which formerly prevented blacks from enjoying full rights as ordinary citizens in the United States. Give examples of the laws and other measures taken by the American Federal government in the 1950s and 1960s to remedy this situation.

6. According to an extract from *The Free Nation*, it has taken communism only 45 years to swallow 27 countries. Give a date for both the start and finish of these 45 years. Name as many of these 27 countries as you can.

7. Attitudes towards the USA and the USSR

(a) A group can divide into two parts. One half lists ten statements about the Americans and the United States while the other half lists ten statements about the Russians and the Soviet Union. The two sections can then discuss and rearrange the statements on other sheets of paper, each headed 'positive', 'negative' and 'neutral'. Statements about the USA could be mounted on one wall and statements about the USSR on the opposite wall to form two charts.

After everyone has studied the various statements the whole group could discuss the general picture which emerges of the two countries.

(b) Small groups could explore in detail relevant points from the chart with reference to the weaknesses and strengths of the USA and USSR respectively. (Reference can be made to material elsewhere, especially in Chapters 4 and 6 of this book.)
They might use of headings as listed below:

| The USA | The USSR |
|---|---|
| Advantages/strengths | Advantages/strengths |
| Disadvantages/weaknesses | Disadvantages/weaknesses |

8. Discuss in some groups the extent to which you agree with each of the statements below. Which statements conflict with others, making it impossible for you to agree with all of the statements? (Refer to the article by V Bukovsky on page 94.)

**Impressions about peace**

Summary of some of the attitudes and opinions about the subject.

(a) Peace is something which we have to continually struggle to attain throughout our lives, just as we have to struggle to prevent ourselves committing sin, crime or misbehaving. When war is ended as a means of settling differences, humanity will have reached maturity and be able to concentrate on the search for real peace.

(b) Most people yearn for world peace and security.

(c) Some people talk as if they wanted peace but are in fact quite happy with a state of tension and occasional wars as it is in their own interests, for instance people who are concerned about their military careers or making profits from arms production and trade.

**(d)** There are some genuine campaigners for peace and human rights in the so-called 'Iron Curtain' countries who must carry on their activities at the risk of imprisonment and loss of personal freedom.

**(e)** The Soviet government's expressed desire for peace is merely a ruse to weaken Western resistance to communism, since their definition of peace is a communist world. The World Peace Council is a Soviet-controlled propaganda vehicle to promote this end.

**(f)** Most Western peace movements are dangerous, being primarily inspired by the desire to weaken the resistance of Western governments to the spread of left-wing ideas or the expansion of communism.

**(g)** Most Western peace movements reflect a genuine concern about world problems and security and a desire to see a better, freer and more secure world.

**(h)** Peace means the absence of fighting or any form of physical violence.

9. Find out more about human rights as promoted by various British political parties. Refer to the 1983 edition of *The Times Guide to the House of Commons* (available in most major libraries) or other sources if necessary.
Name the political party which at the 1983 and/or subsequent election supported each of the following: **(a)** Animal Rights Charter **(b)** a new Bill of Rights Act **(c)** a decentralised and nuclear-free Europe **(d)** ending a multi-racial Britain.

10. List important aspects of American and Russian electoral procedures. Later discuss in pairs the relative strengths and defects of both systems. Role-play an American and Russian defending their respective procedures.

# 12 WORLD PROBLEMS AND PREPARATION FOR THE FUTURE

## 12.1   The Need for Greater World Co-operation

Many of the world's problems are closely interrelated and need to be viewed and treated as such. In contrast, matters such as starvation, overpopulation, disease and destruction of the environment, tend to be handled in a piecemeal manner, with separate organisations dealing with each aspect. In addition, problems in one part of the world easily affect people elsewhere, so that long-term security, well-being and survival depends on all countries and peoples working together to find joint solutions. An example was the accident at Chernobyl, near Kiev in the USSR, on 26 April 1986, where the explosion of a nuclear reactor eventually led to fall-out contaminating more than 20 countries.

Just as all parts of a human being are interrelated, or all the parts of a car are locked together into a single system, so vegetation, water and the atmosphere are interrelated, so that adverse activity in one area affects others. Thus a need thus arises for greater control or regulation on a world scale for such things as oil spills, air pollution and the handling of radioactive waste.

---

The earth is one country and all people are its citizens.

*Baháu'lláh*

---

### When Co-operation Makes Sense

Sometimes rival groups find it advantageous to unite against common dangers or to solve urgent problems.

The Sunday Times, *17 February 1980*

## THE ROBBER'S CAVE EXPERIMENT

Groups sometimes resolve their differences if they find that they have to co-operate to achieve some common goal that cannot be achieved by either group alone. For purposes of research, Muzafer Sherif and his colleagues gave competing groups of boys, who had come to dislike each other, situations which involved their working together in order to survive. It was found that they eventually joined forces in common tasks, and that this led to a reduction in tension and a growth of understanding and an appreciation of the good points of the other side.

*Muzafer Sherif,* Intergroup Conflict and Cooperation: the Robber's Cave Experiment, *1961*

**Reduction of the nuclear war threat**   After many years of distrusting each other the Soviet Union and the Western powers (the USA, Britain and France) became allies in 1941 after the Nazi invasion of Russia. Once a common danger is removed there is always the risk that allies may fall out with each other and renew old rivalries. This happened in 1945 when the Cold War put an end to wartime allied co-operation. However, both superpowers have common interests in preventing a nuclear holocaust.

# CO-OPERATION

## IS BETTER THAN CONFLICT

*Quaker Peace and Service*

Understanding, love and tolerance are the highest forms of interest on our small and interdependent planet.

*U Thant*

**Common interests versus national interests: the examples of the ocean**   In December 1982, under the auspices of the third UN conference on the sea 'Unclos', the Law of the Sea treaty was signed by 119 countries. This set up the International Seabed Authority (ISA) to regulate the exploitation of the seabed's mineral resources for the benefit of everyone. All the waters outside the 200 mile exclusive economic zones (EEZs) are covered. Within these coastal zones states have, since the late 1970s, claimed 'sovereign rights' to exploit the resources.

The Seabed Treaty had to be ratified by at least 60 countries within two years before it became binding international law. Twenty-two of the world's industrialised countries, including the United States, Japan, Britain and West Germany, refused to sign the treaty. Yet these are the countries with the technological knowledge and money necessary to make the seabed project a success. The United States, for example, fears that the treaty will restrict private enterprise and the activities of multinational mining companies, and that it will lose control of vital strategic resources which are within its capacity to exploit, such as manganese, cobalt, copper and nickel. In addition, the present US government under President Reagan fears that it will mean a reduction of American economic and political influence and make the USA liable to political blackmail if the new ISA was controlled by a majority hostile to its interests.

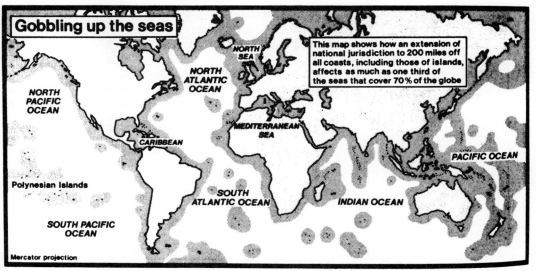

The Economist, *13 May 1978*

## ACTIVITIES

1. Find out recent details about the Law of the Sea treaty and Unclos.

2. Why is the world now showing more interest in the oceans? Does the difficulty of states in reaching agreement concerning rights to develop the oceans symbolise problems of getting countries to co-operate in general for the common good?

In 1854, 'the Great White Chief' in Washington made an offer for a large area of Indian land and promised a 'reservation' for the Indian people. The reply of Chief Seattle of the Suquamish Nation, extracts of which are given overleaf, has been described as the most beautiful and profound statement on the environment ever made.

How can you buy or sell the sky, the warmth of the land? The idea is strange to us.

If we do not own the freshness of the air and the sparkle of the water, how can you buy them?

So, when the Great Chief in Washington sends word that he wishes to buy our land, he asks much of us. The Great Chief sends word he will reserve us a place so that we can live comfortably to ourselves.

He will be our father and we will be his children. So we will consider your offer to buy our land.

But it will not be easy. For this land is sacred to us.

## One Condition

So we will consider your offer to buy our land. If we decide to accept, I will make one condition: the white man must treat the beasts of this land as his brothers. I am a savage and I do not understand any other way.

I have seen a thousand rotting buffaloes on the prairie, left by the white man who shot them from a passing train.

I am a savage and I do not understand how the smoking iron horse can be more important than the buffalo that we kill only to stay alive.

What is man without the beasts? If all the beasts were gone, man would die from a great loneliness of spirit. For whatever happens to the beasts, soon happens to man. All things are connected.

## The Ashes

You must teach your children that the ground beneath their feet is the ashes of your grandfathers. So that they will respect the land, tell your children that the earth is rich with the lives of our kin.

Teach your children what we have taught our children, that the earth is our mother.

Whatever befalls the earth befalls the sons of the earth. If men spit upon the ground, they spit upon themselves.

This we know: the earth does not belong to man, man belongs to the earth. This we know.

All things are connected like the blood which unites one family. All things are connected.

Whatever befalls the earth befalls the sons of the earth. Man did not weave the web of life: he is merely a strand in it. Whatever he does to the web, he does to himself.

One thing we know, which the white man may one day discover – our God is the same God.

You may think now that you own Him as you wish to own our land; but you cannot. He is the God of man, and His compassion is equal for the red man and the white.

This earth is precious to Him, and to harm the earth is to heap contempt on its Creator.

The whites too shall pass; perhaps sooner than all other tribes. Contaminate your bed, and you will one night suffocate in your own waste.

Answer the following questions based on the extract on pages 197–8:

1. How does the extract show differences in attitude to life and culture between the American Indian and the white man?

2. Illustrate how the extract shows the tolerance, lack of prejudice and broad-mindedness of the Chief.

3. Explain how the Chief describes relations between people and their environment as if they were all parts of a system or machine.

4. Which passage in the context is close in meaning to the Old Testament book Leviticus 25: 30 'Land belongs to God'?

5. Explain the meaning of the following phrase: 'If men spit upon the ground, they spit upon themselves'.

## Advantages of the System of States

No alternative system has yet been found by which people can be governed and society organised. Giuseppe Mazzini, the Italian nationalist, argued that each person's duties were first to humanity, then to his or her country and family. However, he argued that only in a nation were the individual and humanity ideally united.

The individual is too weak, and humanity too vast. 'My God,' prays the Breton mariner as he puts out to sea, 'protect me, my ship is so little and Thy ocean so great!' And this prayer sums up the condition of each of you, if no means is found of multiplying your forces and your powers of action indefinitely. But God gave you this means when He gave you a country, when, like a wise overseer of labour, who distributes the different parts of the work according to the capacities of the workmen, he divided humanity into distinct groups upon the face of the globe, and thus planted the seeds of nations.

*G Mazzini*, The Duties of Man, *1907*

Note that Mazzini assumed, as did many Europeans, that it would be natural and just to merge the two ideas together, a nation and a state, so forming a 'nation state'. In other words, the French would live in France, the Italians in a united Italian state, and the Germans in Germany, and there would be an end to multinational empires such as the Habsburg and Ottoman Empires. (See Chapter 3, pages 53–4.)

It was the considerable strength of the nation state idea that led many in the past and the present to talk as if the 'nation' is in fact identical with the 'state', as you will see in the following quotation.

If I knew of a thing useful to my nation but ruinous to another I would not propose it to my prince, because I am a man before being French, (or again) because I am of necessity a man, and only French by chance.

*Montesquieu, 1689–1755*

'The Big Three, 1985', Daily Telegraph, *7 May 1985*

## Disadvantages of the States System

**1.**  Aggressive nationalism or 'jingoism' can lead to a desire to dominate others. This was a factor in the creation of colonial empires by Britain, France, Spain, the Netherlands and Portugal, and briefly by the USA.

**2.**  Despite the notion of state sovereignty, states are unequal in power and resources and so the weaker are vulnerable, not really self-supporting, making them dependent on others.

3. Governments in many states do not properly perform one of their basic functions of protecting a citizen's security and welfare, and instead widespread oppression and violation of human rights may occur. This is particularly the case where minorities or individuals face persecution or discrimination on religious, political or racial grounds.

4. The states system is unable to adapt quickly enough to modern developments. States have not yet been able to work together to solve pressing world problems such as the nuclear threat, the growth of international violence and terrorism, unemployment and pollution and the destruction of the environment.

---

In the long run [people] are going to do more for peace than are governments. Indeed, I think that people want peace so much that one of these days governments had better get out of the way and let them have it.

*President Eisenhower*

---

## ACTIVITIES

1. In which one of the following countries did the nuclear accident at Three Mile Island, Harrisburg (1978) occur: **(a)** Sweden **(b)** Britain **(c)** France **(d)** West Germany **(e)** United States?

2. Suggest a suitable caption for the picture from *The Sunday Times* (page 195), incorporating one of the following words: **(a)** boat **(b)** spaceship **(c)** village **(d)** community.

3. Look at the cartoon 'The Big Three, 1985' (page 200).

   **(a)** Name the three leaders looking on from the clouds, and the famous meeting they had in 1945.

   **(b)** In what way can the cartoon be related to one of the weaknesses of the states system today?

   **(c)** Do you agree that the three main problems today are as described in the cartoon? In what way might 'unemployment', 'arms control' and 'terrorism' reflect symptoms or the effects of problems, rather than the actual problems we face today?

4. Discover details of the work of four of the specialised agencies of the United Nations, and of how they are trying to overcome some of the world's problems today.

5. Construct a web chart showing the links between injustice, destruction of the environment, selfishness and differing beliefs and those problems listed below. Alternatively, design your own web chart showing the relationship between some of the main problems affecting the world today.

(a) poverty
(b) unemployment
(c) population explosion
(d) physical violence
(e) nuclear arms race
(f) arms trade
(g) intolerance (political, religious, etc)
(h) discrimination, for example sexism, racism
(i) sickness and disease
(j) illiteracy
(k) materialism
(l) mistrust

## 12.2 Possible Futures

Most of the various suggestions which have been made as to how to achieve greater world unity, or how the world will or should resolve its problems are covered under the three main categories below:

**1. Grouping together models** Some people support the eventual creation of a world authority or government which would have the power to enforce decisions as national governments have today. This would imply that all states had disarmed, except for the retention of light weapons to preserve domestic peace.

A world system might be based on a reformed United Nations in which existing countries were represented according to population size. The world authority would be supported by global agencies, created out of the existing UN specialised agencies such as the World Health Organisation (WHO) which would help achieve a more equitable system of distribution of the world's resources. A global peacekeeping force, consisting of volunteers financed by tax on member states would protect all states against attack.

Progress might be made towards this model through the linking together of existing supra-national organisations such as the European Community (or Common Market), and the Council for Mutual Economic Assistance (COMECON) in Eastern Europe, or the strengthening of loose organisations such as the Organisation of African Unity. As people of many countries co-operated more in joint activities together, they might acquire a greater attachment to regional identities or to the world as a whole.

**2. Smaller group models** Other people have argued that there are too many large impersonal centralised organisations in the world, whether states or multinational businesses. Fritz Schumacher has popularised the idea that 'small is beautiful' and that people can only really participate in an organisation that is much smaller than many of the states that exist today. In addition a world of small political units of about 5–10 million inhabitants would make it easier for each unit to agree on how a loose global authority

*The Peacable Kingdom by the American artist Edward Hicks (1780–1849), based on Isaiah's prophecy of peace between all living things*

could make rules for activities of common interest, such as the safeguarding of the oceans, or the regulation of air pollution. In such a world an individual might have greater freedom to live and migrate as he or she wanted.

**3. Alternative Lifestyles**  Opponents of the present way of life in the Western world argued that it encourages a high level of consumption, profit-making and the search for ever higher living standards, which results in waste, the extravagant use of scarce resources, and the widening of differences between the rich and poor in the world. A shift towards 'no-growth' will help protect the environment, allow poorer countries a fairer share of resources and allow a community to develop goods and services of benefit to all.

Dr F E Trainer, an Australian, has written that if the limits to grow argument is correct (see section 4.2) then major changes should be made as suggested below.

---

(a) Buy and consume far less than we do now, which means we must greatly reduce the production of unnecessary things like sports cars and soft drinks.

(b) Produce many more things for ourselves at home, especially food, clothing, furniture, repairs.

(c) Make neighbourhoods more productive, e.g. by having a community work-shop on each block where we can make things, meet, exchange crops, etc. We should have many small market gardens and orchards within suburban areas.

(d) Organise many things ourselves at the neighbourhood level, like rosters, to look after parks and build and maintain windmills, storage sheds, gardens, duck ponds, etc.

(e) Have many community-owned things, like fruit trees, animal pens, wind-mills, tools, swimming pools, which we share.

**(f)** Use alternative technologies like solar panels, windmills, organic gardening, recycling of wastes to compost heaps and garbage gas units, tree crops, building houses from earth.

**(g)** Because these changes would greatly reduce the need for production in factories we could close down many factories, therefore reducing resource use, boring work, travel to work, the number of cars necessary, etc. We might only need two days work a week in factories and offices; we might be able to dig up many roads and plant more gardens.

*F E Trainer, 'Critical Social Issues — Topic I', The Limits to Growth, 1984*

---

G K Chesterton once observed that modern man had not only lost the way but lost the map. Today, only one thing about the future of humanity seems clear: that man has no idea where he is going.

*Arthur Bryant, 1969*

---

## False Needs, Consumerism and Materialism

**Copy cats**  Some thinkers such as Herbert Marcuse, author of *One Dimensional Man* (1964), argue that the vast majority of people remain far below their potential since they seek the satisfaction of false needs, conforming to what others do, or are too influenced by advertising.

Examples are:

- Obsession with accumulating material possessions, rather than in seeking aesthetic, moral satisfaction from nature and art which belong to all (the idea of 'having' rather than 'being').

- Obsession with obtaining power or domination over others, or of socially 'keeping up with, or surpassing, the Joneses', rather than with using power creatively or seeking worthwhile pursuits. — Genuine culture replaced by cheap forms of entertainment, the chief purpose of which is to 'kill time'.

## THE BALL GAME

Sometimes in my naivety I have thought that we might reach a sort of plateau of needs and would all be happy; but when our Abbot went over to the United States to visit a new Benedictine House there, he stayed with a priest in New York who had four television sets in his dining room – one on each wall – in order that they would watch a ball game during supper without having to turn round. So perhaps there is really no plateau to our needs and our growth.

*Thomas Cullinan*, The Roots of Social Injustice, *1973*

There are two ways to get enough. One is to continue to accumulate more and more. The other is to desire less.

*G K Chesterton*

Harare, Zimbabwe – Bevill Packer jumps up and down on his paper tables and dashes his paper chairs to the floor. They are often stronger than wood, he declares, and they help save trees and energy.

Packer, 70, a retired college lecturer, is a proponent of a craft he developed in the late 1970s and dubbed 'appropriate paper-based technology' (APT) – making things out of waste paper.

Today, Packer's products, ranging from tables to toys to bowls to baskets, furnish schools and homes in rural Zimbabwe. His latest product, a paper wheelchair, is being tried out at a home for disabled children. Packer has even used scrap paper to make solar ovens with fronts made of glass collected from junk dealers.

"The beauty of it all is that all APT articles contain at least 99% waste paper" Packer said in an interview. Materials to make the items cost virtually nothing, their manufacture provides employment and they promote conservation." Saving trees is of benefit in Africa, where about 80% of the energy is derived from wood. In Zimbabwe, many rural women spend half the day gathering firewood for cooking and deplete the forests in the process.

*'An Alternative Carpenter in Zimbabwe', Michell Faul,* Herald Tribune, *26 November 1985*

# Effective Aid to Help the Poor

The World Bank, an agency of the United Nations, is one of the main ways through which aid for development is transferred from rich countries to the poor. The Bank has been criticised, as well as Western countries such as the USA, since much of the past aid only benefited the richer elements in the poorer countries and primarily involved large expensive projects such as the building of dams which barely affected the lives of the poor, especially in rural areas.

In the last ten years the Bank has concentrated on aid designed to reduce population growth and to help directly the poor such as improving basic health services, introducing better nutrition, increasing literacy and promoting a more even income distribution. Aid has been given to very poor countries either as loans at very low rates of interest for long-term periods (up to 50 years) or in some cases as interest-free loans.

**UNITED NATIONS**     Punch, *11 February 1963*

**New International Economic Order (NIEDO)**   This was proposed by the developing countries at a special meeting of the United Nations in April 1974. Various countries have had conflicting ideas as to what **NIEDO** means. Some have argued that it would include the following measures:

**1.**   The cancellation of some of the huge debts of the developing world

**2.**   The transfer of resources from the rich to the poor countries, to be given as compensation for past and present exploitation of the poor by the rich countries.

---

Imagine all the people living for today
Imagine there are no countries it isn't hard to do, Nothing to kill or die for and no religion too.
Imagine all the people living life in peace.
You may say I'm a dreamer,
But I'm not the only one;
I hope some day you'll join us
And the world will be as one.

*John Lennon*

---

## ACTIVITIES

**1.**   Answer true or false to the following statements:

**(a)** '"Small is beautiful" means that the world should only have one strong army, a UN peace force, and all other armies would be disbanded.' If you disagree, say what you think 'small is beautiful' means.

**(b)** 'One advantage of the alternative society is that it is an attempt to reduce extravagance and waste.'

**(c)** 'According to the philosophy of Marcuse, a 'walkman' would be an example of the satisfaction of a false need.'

**(d)** 'Most people agree that today we have more or less reached the limit of our needs and the end to growth.'

**(e)** 'Windmills are an energy-saving mechanism.' If you disagree say why. If you agree, name any other mechanisms you think might save energy.

**2.**   Suggest two reasons why rich and poor countries would have difficulty in reaching agreement on the nature of a New International Economic Order.

**3.**   Discover examples of world co-operation outside the United Nations in various specific areas such as health, transport and communications. For example, look at the career of Florence Nightingale and discover when and why the International Red Cross was founded.

4. If our technical way of life collapsed in the future, how many items would you not be able to use? Explain how you would manage to live without them. Identify communities in parts of the world which do without most if not all of these items at present.

5. Construct a time line, putting in five main events which have happened from 1970 to the present. Then extend the time line by adding:

**(a)** five preferable things you would like to see

**(b)** five probable things which you think are likely to happen

**(c)** five things you would not want to see in the future. If necessary these might include items from (b)

**(d)** How you would plan to get to your preferred world.

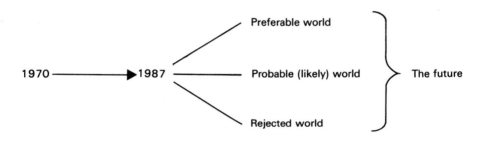

6. What does the cartoon from *Oxfam News* (below) teach us about the interdependence of countries? A class project can be organised around discovering the origin of certain items. For example, the local departmental store could be visited for inquiries about the origins of ten manufactured articles. Find items which have come from various parts of the EEC, other parts of Europe or the world. Or note ten key items in your classroom and discover their origins, then find out the origin of most shoes, typewriters and motor cars.

Ian Kellas, Oxfam News, *May 1984*

7. Hold a class discussion about the value or use of the various proposals outlined in this section concerning the future. Which one or two would the majority prefer? Discuss any possible modifications or improvements to any of the proposals, or better alternatives. (Perhaps a brainstorming session could help initially, so that ideas can be gathered quickly from the group.)

8. Find at least 16 words hidden in this letter square, reading horizontally, vertically or diagonally only. Then make up your own letter square based on concepts and ideas from this book or a particular chapter. Now swap these with those made by your neighbours and find the words in their letter squares.

| C | A | R | I | N | G | R | F |
| L | O | V | E | S | A | P | A |
| W | T | N | B | E | R | A | M |
| I | E | E | F | O | T | X | I |
| N | J | A | R | L | M | A | N |
| W | A | R | P | R | I | B | E |
| M | E | A | N | O | O | C | S |
| T | R | U | S | T | N | R | T |

9. Each person could collect over a period of a month items from the press or elsewhere which refer to means by which the world might achieve greater unity. Then hold a group thinking session with suggested items being listed on the board. At the end the group can discuss the relative importance of each item or this can be done by dividing the group into smaller groups. Items could be classified into four categories as shown on the right.

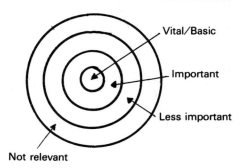

Vital/Basic

Important

Less important

Not relevant

10. Drama session. The class could divide into small groups. Each group has to mime or perform silently:

(a) something which they think is bad or unfortunate about the world or society they live in today;

(b) something which they would like to see happen in the future.

The rest of the class could try to guess the theme or the idea that the groups tried to portray. The class could organise the details of how best to carry out this general suggestion. Naturally this type of activity can be adapted, and might take the form of short sketches or charades.

# Organisations

*Key:*

| | | | |
|---|---|---|---|
| D | – Development | WS | – World Studies/Future Studies |
| HR | – Human Rights | S/D | – Security/Disarmament |
| P | – Peace | IU | – International Understanding |
| P(M) | – Peace materials/syllabus | E | – Environment |
| R | – Resource Centre | | |

| | |
|---|---|
| HR | Amnesty International, 5 Roberts Place, off Bowling Green Lane, London EC1 OEJ |
| HR | Animal Aid, 7 Castle Street, Tonbridge, Kent TN9 IBH |
| P(M) | British Atlantic Committee, 30a St James's Square, London SW1Y 4JH |
| S/D | Campaign Against the Arms Trade, 11 Goodwin Street, London N4 3HQ |
| S/D | Campaign for Nuclear Disarmament (CND), 22–4 Underwood Street, London N1 7JQ |
| IU | Catholic Institute for International Relations (CIIR), 1 Cambridge Terrace, London NW1 4JL |
| R | Central Film Library, Chalfont Grove, Gerrards Cross, Buckinghamshire, S19 8TN |
| WS | Centre for Alternative Technology, Llwyngwern Quarry, Machynlleth, Powys, Wales |
| D | Centre for World Development Education (CWDE), 128 Buckingham Palace Road, London SW1W 9SH |
| D | Christian Aid, PO Box 1, London SW9 8BH |
| HR | Compassion in World Farming, 20 Lavant Street, Petersfield, Hants GU32 3JG |
| R | Concord Films Council, 201 Felixstowe Road, Ipswich, Suffolk IP3 9BJ |
| IU | Council for Education in World Citizenship, Mews House, Seymour Mews, London W1H 9PE |
| E | European Group for Ecological Action (ECOROPA), c/o Gerard Morgan-Grenville, Crickhowell, Powys NP8 ITA |
| S/D | European Nuclear Disarmament (END), Bertrand Russell House, Gamble Street, Nottingham NG7 4ET |
| P | Fellowship of Reconciliation (FOR), 40–6 Harleyford Road, London SE11 5AY |
| HR | Freedom Association, Avon House, 360–6 Oxford Street, London WIN OAA |
| E | Friends of the Earth, 377 City Road, London EC1V 1NA |
| R | Housmans Bookshop, 5 Caledonian Road, London N1 9DX |

| | |
|---|---|
| HR | International Society for Human Rights, (British Section), 56 Sutherland Street, London SW1 |
| P | Irish Commission for Justice and Peace, 169 Booterstown Avenue, Blackrock, Co Dublin |
| HR | Minority Rights Group, Benjamin Franklin House, 36 Craven Street, London WC2N 5NG |
| S/D | National Council for Civil Defence, 21 Selan Gardens, Hayes, Middlesex UB4 OEA |
| HR | National Council for Civil Liberties, 21 Tabard Street, London SE1 |
| D | New Internationalist, 42 Hythe Bridge Street, Oxford OX1 2EP |
| P(M) | Nottingham Association for Peace Education, 16 Ebers Road, Mappeley Park, Nottingham |
| E | Nuclear Information, P.O. Box 11, Godalming, Surrey |
| D | Oxfam, 274 Banbury Road, Oxford, OX2 7DZ |
| P | Pax Christi, St Francis of Assisi Centre, Pottery Lane, London W11 4NQ |
| P | Peace Education Network, c/o Gil Fell, 11 Alexandra Road South, Whalley Range, Manchester M16 8GE |
| P | Peace Pledge Union, Dick Sheppard House, 6 Endsleigh Street, London |
| P | Quaker Peace and Service, Friends House, Euston Road, London NW1 2BJ |
| IU | United Nations Association, 3 Whitehall Court, London SW1A 2EL |
| IU | United Nations Information Centre, 20 Buckingham Gate, London SW1E 6LB |
| D | War on Want, 467 Caledonian Road, London N7 9BE |
| S/D | World Disarmament Campaign, 238 Camden Road, London NW1 9HE |
| WS | World Studies Project, 24 Palace Chambers, Bridge Street, London SW1A 2JT |

A useful resource book (with suggested activities including case studies and role plays) is:

Anne Wilkinson, *It's not fair – a handbook on world development for youth groups*, Christian Aid, 1985

# INDEX